Praise for The Butcher, The Baker, The Candlestick Maker

'It was so hot, I just wanted to stop reading and have sex,'
Cosmopolitan

'For once an author has got it right . . . Book of the Month,'
Scarlet

'Ravenous, sexually charged,' *Men's Health*

'Intelligently written (and) brutally honest,' *Metro*

'Eye-poppingly unambiguous prose,' *Esquire*

'Gritty and Explicit,' *The Observer*

'As mind-boggling as it is shocking,' *The Mirror*

'The woman who has it all has it off,' *Word Magazine*

'Breathy and explicit,' *The Jewish Chronicle*

Also by Suzanne Portnoy

The Butcher, The Baker, The Candlestick Maker

THE NOT SO INVISIBLE WOMAN

Suzanne Portnoy

First published in Great Britain in 2008 by
Virgin Books
Thames Wharf Studios
Rainville Road
London W6 9HA

Distributed in the USA by Holtzbrinck Publishers, LLC,
175 Fifth Avenue, New York, NY 10010, USA

The Random House Group Limited supports The Forest
Stewardship Council [FSC], the leading international forest
certification organisation. All our titles that are printed on
Greenpeace approved FSC certified paper carry the FSC logo.
Our paper procurement policy can be found at
www.rbooks.co.uk/environment

Mixed Sources
Product group from well-managed
forests and other controlled sources
www.fsc.org Cert no. TT-COC-002227
© 1996 Forest Stewardship Council
FSC

ISBN 978 0 7535 1395 8

Typeset by Phoenix Photosetting, Chatham, Kent
Printed and bound by CPI Bookmarque, Croydon, Surrey

1 3 5 7 9 10 8 6 4 2

ACKNOWLEDGEMENTS

To Michael O'Loughlin – collaborator, friend, editor, confidant – without whom this book would not have been possible.

To Adam Nevill at Virgin Books – for his advice and support.

To my kids – for putting up with having an 'original' mum.

To Carol – for being a great chum.

To the Perverts Tea Saloon – for being so welcoming when I came to NYC.

To Selina Fire – my fellow partner in crime.

To my folks – who have always been so loving and wonderful.

And to all the guys who gave and still give me so much pleasure.

Some names and situations have been changed to protect identities.

The author is aware that the websites and publications mentioned did not and could not control her interaction with members.

'Never be afraid to laugh at yourself. After all, you could be missing out on the joke of the century.'

– Dame Edna Everage, a.k.a. Barry Humphries

PROLOGUE

The infamous American radio shock jock Howard Stern recently said, 'If you want to have sex with women, date a divorced woman with young children. Because every other weekend, the husband has the kids, and that means every two weeks she gets to go out for one night – and go berserk.'

Actually, that was me he was talking about. And he's right. At least, he's right about me. Though he got one point wrong – there are actually *two* kids-free nights every other weekend.

I got divorced seven years ago, after a mostly sexless marriage that lasted a decade. Since then, I've been making up for lost time – though I have had a few monogamous relationships along the way, mostly disastrous ones, with guys who cheated on me or who treated my wallet like it was their own. But sexual freedom, I also learned, didn't necessarily lead to happiness, even if it did tend to come with an orgasm. All things considered, however, I've still come to the conclusion that I am happiest when I don't have *one* man in my life, but several.

These days, I rotate a portfolio of men, each of whom I meet every two weeks or so for fun. When one drops out, I find another, mainly via the internet, where there's a fertile supply of good-looking, nice, frisky guys who, like me, aren't looking for a relationship and just want to have good sex. I'm not discounting the idea that some day I might find The One, but I've stopped looking. Now, I just look for fun.

I'm having a good time. I've met some interesting men and some not-so-interesting men. Some of their stories follow. I hope you enjoy my kiss-and-tells.

1. THE COCK DOC

It was just after 9 a.m. when the doorbell rang.

I ran downstairs from my bedroom, adjusting my stockings, and opened the door. I had delayed my cleaning lady's arrival by one hour, and was relieved to see a tall attractive man in a white coat standing on my front step, and not Anna. He held a leather briefcase in one hand and a stethoscope hung around his neck. 'You must be Doctor Donny,' I said.

'That's me.' He looked up and down my body, then met my eyes and smiled. 'May I come in?'

'Follow me,' I said, and turned back into the hall. 'I assume you wish to examine me in the bedroom, doctor.' I walked up the stairs without looking behind me.

I led him to my bedroom, then shut the door, in case Anna had not picked up the message I'd left the previous evening.

'Clothed or unclothed?' I asked.

He looked over at me while putting his briefcase on the Chinese trunk at the foot of my bed. 'I think unclothed is best,' he said matter-of-factly, in a deep voice I found alluring. He spoke as if he'd been asked that question a thousand times.

'Would you like me to remove my underwear, doctor?' I asked, trying to sound nonchalant to disguise my nervousness. I've had dozens of strangers in my bed, men whose names I barely knew, but usually I met playmates in public places and checked them out before inviting them home. I'd never had a house call before.

'Yes,' he said, authoritatively. 'But you can keep your bra on.'

I unbuttoned my shrug, pulled off my T-shirt and unzipped my skirt. Looking away, I slowly slid my knickers down to my ankles. I stepped out of the knickers, making sure to keep my transparent bra, stockings and high lace-up heels in place. I felt like a cross between Miss Jean Brodie and an Agent Provocateur model. Slowly, I folded my clothing, placed it carefully on the trunk and lay down on my bed. I felt the high of anticipation mixed with the excitement that comes only when I'm being touched by a stranger for the first time.

Dr Donny put the stethoscope to his ears, moved towards me and placed the tip of the instrument over my pubic area. I had shaved the night before, leaving just a small rectangle of hair, and the instrument felt cold against my skin. I was more amused than aroused. I had never heard of a stethoscope being used to gauge the health of a woman's pussy. This was not the doctor fantasy I had in mind.

'Mmmmn,' said Dr Donny, continuing to manoeuvre his stethoscope around my pubic area. 'Your pussy sounds healthy enough.' His tone remained authoritative, just the way professionals speak in a medical centre. I tried not to laugh. The tone was fine but the action was all wrong.

Dr Donny pulled the stethoscope out of his ears, put it beside his briefcase and resumed his examination using his hands. He placed his long fingers on either side of my labia, spread open the lips, and rubbed his fingers in a small circle around my clitoris. 'You have a lovely pussy,' he said.

'Thank you, doctor.' I felt myself getting wet. Then, rather too quickly, I felt a warm tongue on my clit. I spread my legs to allow him easier access.

'I think I need to get you wetter,' he said, suddenly adopting a seductive tone, before carrying on with his oral investigation.

Dr Donny was standing beside me, leaning over while eating me out. His tongue continued to massage my clit for a few disconcerting minutes. It felt good, but as I lay back and let him carry on, I felt a slight twinge of regret that this handsome, dark-haired man was no longer behaving like a real gynaecologist. He was just another stranger in my bed. But I made the most of it and relaxed into the sensations.

I let him carry on for a few minutes. Then I turned my head and saw, just above eye level, Dr Donny's hard-on straining against the fly of his black trousers. Impressive. I reached across to feel his cock through the fabric. It felt large and fat and hard.

Feeling my hand on his crotch, Dr Donny stood up. 'Would you like to have a look?' he asked.

'Yes, please,' I whispered, trying to stay in character as the submissive patient.

Slowly he undid his belt and unzipped his fly, and released one of the most perfect cocks I'd ever seen. It had been two weeks since I'd seen one, and this was a great reintroduction to the species. I slid my hand around the thick shaft. Then I sat up from the bed, pulled his cock towards my eager lips, and took it inside my mouth. I felt hands on the back of my head, pushing me down the shaft. It was far too big to take in my throat.

I didn't want to gag, so I pulled back and began stroking the base of his cock whilst licking and sucking the head.

'That is very good,' he said, resuming a professional tone. 'Very good indeed.'

That made me laugh. Clearly, we weren't playing doctor and patient any more.

I was a little disappointed that the curtain had fallen on our little drama so quickly. I had expected more role-playing, had wanted my fantasy doctor to touch and grope and explore my body for more than just that two-minute stethoscope scene. I'd woken up feeling horny and antsy with anticipation. I had wanted to play out the doctor–patient scenario for many years.

The hot doctor's visit was one of the few boxes left on my fantasy list that hadn't been ticked. For as long as this fantasy had been on my mind, I'd had girlfriends who'd giggled about their own. While most of them kept their dirty dreams locked up, unrealised, I learned to act on mine, even if their outcomes often proved less satisfying than my imagination.

I had planned simply to lie back and be used and probed like a patient on the gurney. It was not my intention to be an active, much less an equal, participant in a sex act that morning. After all, sex was nothing new for me. The doctor–patient scenario, however, was new – and long overdue. I'd been to orgies and sex clubs, hooked up with hundreds of strangers and fuck buddies before, and today I was hoping to finally fulfil my number one fantasy – of being completely passive and submitting to another's control and authority and expertise. Even a fake doctor's expertise.

While sucking Dr Donny's cock, and enjoying it, I concluded that probably I should have been clearer about my doctor fantasy when I arranged it. The fixation had popped into my head a decade earlier, out of the blue while masturbating, and it had remained there, unfulfilled, ever since. So when, the night before, I was asked about my sexual fantasies while chatting with guys on Swinging Heaven, I took the opportunity to toss the idea out there. I'd waited too long for this doctor's appointment.

Swinging Heaven is my favourite hook-up site, my one-stop shop for quick cock. Either because I'm a long-time user or one of the few genuine single women on the site, I get a free membership.

After my divorce in 2001, I decided that until I found a man with whom I could truly be myself, I'd just have fun. Like me, and unlike too many of my previous boyfriends, the new men in my life would have to have moved beyond the idea of monogamy. I didn't believe in it and didn't intend to practise it – at least in terms of sex. I have a monogamous heart but very different standards when it comes to my body. So unless I met my soulmate, I decided, I'd have fun with a portfolio of guys who wanted to have some fun of their own. Most of them, I discovered, were on Swinging Heaven. When I'm on the lookout for a new man to fill an empty space, with a few strokes of the keyboard, I can see exactly what's on offer.

In the 'Jacuzzi' chat room a man named Donny introduced himself. His face pic was blurred, but not so blurry that I couldn't tell he was attractive, dark haired, and in his mid to late thirties. I pulled up his profile to check out his cock. The first photo showed a well-tanned man with broad shoulders and an attractive Mediterranean-looking face. He was wearing a loose white linen shirt similar to one that Daniel, an ex-boyfriend of mine, had pretty much lived in until it turned to shreds after four years. Daniel also was broad and dark and Mediterranean looking, as was my ex-husband, David. Which is to say, Donny was just my type. Or had the potential to be. My type is also well hung, and in his profile Donny advertised a nine-inch cock. So I checked out his other photos. He wasn't lying. Up popped a photo of a baton of a cock, standing bolt upright, almost parallel to his chest. I wanted to meet him.

'Nice cock.'

'thanks would u like 2 meet it'

'Love to. I'm feeling horny as hell.'

We began to discuss interests and he asked me about my fantasies. I told him I had a lot, most of them pretty stupid and typical: being gang-banged, being cast in a porn movie and having to show the director how tight and deep my pussy is – pretty run-of-the-mill stuff.

'hot'

'My number one fantasy is that I'm having an internal

examination by a handsome male doctor and he uses his cock as the speculum.'

'i have a white coat,' Donny wrote back, 'and a stethoscope ;)'

'Really?' I was surprised and instantly excited at the direction this chat was taking. Usually I didn't participate in chats and instead just watched guys wank live and issued instructions. I regularly told guys to play with their balls, to lick their pre-come, to play with their nipples. It was a turn-on to be the director of the action and not the subject of it, and guys liked it, too.

'really. what do u say i cum round to yr place n give u a checkup'

'Sometimes I have breakfast meetings,' I wrote. I could drop my kids off at school and be home by nine. 'I just so happen to have an opening tomorrow morning. Do you have an appointment free at that time?'

'it just so happens that i do,' he replied. 'call me dr Donny. i'll bring my 9 inch equipment.'

Those nine inches were crucial because, when I see a real gyno, they always take out the largest speculum available. I've always been told that I have an almost abnormally deep vagina.

My ultimate doctor fantasy is actually a threesome, with a hot male doctor and a sexy female nurse. I'm lying helpless on an examination table with my legs in stirrups, and a female nurse with great tits and a low-cut uniform is massaging my clit. She's preparing me for the doctor, who'll use his own cock as a speculum.

I knew it was ridiculous, but I got off on the thought of a doctor sliding his cock in and out of me in an attempt to ascertain, to his satisfaction, whether or not I was orgasmic. That was a new twist on my theme. I had read a book about the history of the vibrator and learned that it had once been a common practice for doctors to vaginally massage patients suffering with 'hysteria'. The aim was to take the hysterics to orgasm and exorcise their excitable nerves. Hysterical or not, the hysterics seemed to like the treatment, because the vibrator was invented as a labour-saving device after the queue at the doctor's office became unmanageable. I wanted the same treatment, plus an attractive doctor-and-nurse combo that could sort me out the old-fashioned way. But in the absence of two representatives of the medical profession, a single Dr Donny would do.

The doctor's appointment made, I signed off from Swinging Heaven and went to bed. I could hardly sleep.

Dr Donny lowered his hands and reached inside my bra and squeezed my nipples hard. 'I think you need an internal examination,' he said. 'Just to make sure your pussy is healthy.'

I concurred, but the doctor fantasy was shot at this point, and all I was thinking about was that big cock filling me up.

I grabbed a condom from my side drawer and handed it over. He pushed it down the length of his cock. I noticed it barely reached the base of his shaft. Dr Donny quickly removed his white coat and the rest of his clothes, and climbed on top of me.

Although my fantasy hadn't turned out to be what I'd expected, just sucking that cock really aroused me. So when he said, 'I need to be inside your pussy,' I was ready and plenty wet. But his cock was so thick, it took four or five thrusts before he could enter me. That was horny, too, knowing I was almost too tight for him. He inched his way in until my vagina gave way and his full length was inside. I felt him reach to near my cervix. It was a rush to be stretched and filled by someone so big.

'Your pussy is so tight,' he said, pumping me. 'I think I need to fuck you every day for it to remain healthy.' Then, as if hearing his own words and what they implied, he quickly amended his prescription. 'Well, maybe three times a week.'

I looked up at him.

'Twice a day,' he added.

I said nothing. Despite the pleasure his treatment sent surging through my body, I quickly came to my senses. There was no way I'd be able to fuck this guy that often, unless I put my kids up for adoption and handed in my notice at work.

Indeed, he would have been lucky for the opportunity to fuck me twice a week. And with a regular dose of that cock of his, I'd have been lucky, too. But with a full-time job and a second career ferrying my two teenagers to their schools and football games, I didn't have much time to sleep with anyone. The occasional morning fuck was my only available appointment, aside from two kids-free weekends a month when I had the house to myself. But, as he was pushing his cock deeper and deeper inside of me, I tried mentally reorganising my calendar to see where I could fit him in. I liked the sex, the way he felt inside me. Then I let the idea go and climbed on top of him, forgetting the practicalities while focusing on my fantasy.

We had been fucking for twenty minutes and still he had a rock-hard erection.

'You make me so hard,' he said. 'You're so horny.'

'Only when I have a big fat cock like yours in my pussy,' I said. My comment wasn't aimed at his ego. I was simply stating a fact. 'And a decent brain too. It's the perfect combo,' I added. Instantly I regretted my words. I was as cool to the concept of the one-off fuck, like most of the guys I met off of Swinging Heaven, but I'd just blown it, sounding like a girlfriend wannabe.

'I'm glad it works for you,' said Dr Donny.

I started grinding down, feeling him deep inside me. I came within minutes. Then I lifted my body off of his and, crouching between his legs, pulled off the condom and then grabbed his cock with my hands. I jerked him off until he came all over his stomach.

As I rubbed the come into his chest, I looked at the clock. Forty minutes had passed since the doorbell chimed.

I lay down next to Dr Donny and wrapped my arms around his chest, noticing for the first time a slight paunch around his middle. I hadn't seen this in his online photo. In fact, he had described himself as 'super fit' and online the body looked tight. But after years of internet dating, I'd grown used to words that weren't true and photos that were dated. At least the cock didn't lie.

I watched his cock go soft as we settled into an after-sex glow that hardly seemed justified. We'd only just met. And yet, in my experience, having sex with a stranger can be just as intimate as sex with someone I've known for years. It takes more than contact. It's a chemical and psychological reaction as much as a physical one. Thirty seconds, thirty years – what's the difference if the brain and the body connect?

'Well, that was nice,' I said, smiling. And I meant it.

'Fantastic!' he said. 'I'm glad you enjoyed my cock.' He smiled.

'You have a beautiful cock,' I said. 'It's the perfect size for me. I didn't even have to think about coming. It just happened. It doesn't always work like that for me.'

'I'm glad I could be of service,' he said, pleased.

I thought about what he had said about fucking me three times a week, and fantasised that he might actually have the time to make it happen.

'Nice house,' he said, looking around my large bedroom. He nodded toward the twenty boxes of high heels stacked against the fireplace. 'I see you like shoes.'

'I need a big house to store all my shoes in,' I joked. I'd had to pay my husband a quarter of a million to keep the place after our divorce, but it had become my refuge. During my marriage, the house often reminded me of my role as hausfrau. Now all mine, it was worth the long hours I put in at my day job at an entertainment company in order to keep it.

'So, doctor, what's your real job?' I asked.

'I run a small hedge fund and work from home about a mile from here.'

Money. Big cock. Local. Does it get more perfect than this?

The only other time I'd met a hedge fund guy was when I went to a party full of them, hosted by *Trader Monthly* magazine and organised by a party-planner mate of mine, Andrew. When Andrew mentioned the event sponsor was Chivas Regal, I decided to go for the drinks. At the last minute my then boyfriend, Karume, insisted on tagging along, on the pretext of making some 'business connections'. He didn't have a job at the time, so I suspected his coming had more to do with his not wanting me to be in the same room as a lot of men with a lot of money. I was his meal ticket. In the four months he lived under my roof, he never brought anything to the table, not even a bottle of cheap wine.

That night, I schmoozed with a dozen multimillionaires at Il Bottaccio, an elegant Georgian mansion turned private club on Grosvenor Place. Karume kept one eye on me and the other on the undernourished models shipped in for the evening as eye candy. As I later realised, juggling a number of women was second nature to him. When I eventually kicked him to the kerb, shortly after the trader party, it was because I discovered he had been sharing his bed with another girl. I wouldn't have minded that, but he had made me give up my own harem when we got together, saying he was 'a one-woman man'.

I was one of the few women at the *Trader Monthly* fête who had a nine-to-five job and sizeable boobs, so was a novelty for the traders, at least those who were actually as interested in brains as in beauty. I learned that, in addition to being loaded, traders could be fun, especially after half a dozen free Chivas cocktails. I picked up the business cards of a couple of attractive guys, before they were snatched away by Karume on the pretext of 'research'. His research never panned out, and I never met another trader until my doctor came calling. After Karume and I broke up, I swore I'd never support another guy ever again and I didn't.

'I have to get to work,' I said.

'Me too.'

Dr Donny and I stood up and began dressing.

I was debating whether to suggest we schedule in another doctor's appointment, when suddenly the doctor beat me to it.

'Listen, I'm going to Monaco in a couple of days for the Grand Prix. Why don't I fly you out for the weekend? We can fuck our brains out there.'

This could be a keeper, I thought. I'd only just met the guy and already he was talking about taking me away somewhere warm and expensive and exotic. Maybe I'd been right about the brain and body connection.

'I'll see if I can move a few things around,' I said. My kids were going to be with their father that weekend, so that wasn't a problem, but I had a client meeting on Friday afternoon that I'd have to rearrange. 'Let me get back to you.'

'Just let me know,' he said. 'I can always book a late ticket.'

We walked downstairs and out onto the street. Dr Donny kissed me on the pavement outside my house. 'Call me,' he said. 'We'll have fun.'

And we would have done, had I ever been given the opportunity to see him again.

I got in the car, put on my Bluetooth, and rang my best mate Nadia, who loved hearing of my exploits.

Nadia is a 43-year-old Lebanese chick with wild dark hair that falls to her shoulders in corkscrew ringlets and a petite, almost boyish body. Thanks to her beauty and olive complexion, she looks a decade younger and often ends up with sexy men who actually are. We met through Karume, whom she fucked before he took up with me. Nadia dated him only briefly, before deciding they weren't sexually compatible. He cleaned out her drinks cabinet and the food in her fridge, but she thought he was fun to have around, if not full time, and their friendship remained solid. We met when Karume took me to Momo Bar, a world music club in the West End, where

Nadia worked as a sound engineer and booked the acts. A fellow Pisces, I liked her immediately. She was amusing and said 'darling' a lot and spoke in dramatic sentences that ended in exclamation points.

'Oh, darling,' said Nadia, as I recounted my appointment with the bogus doctor, 'had you met this man before?'

'Only on the web,' I said.

'And you let him into your house? Are you crazy?'

I told her he was a hedge-fund trader who lived down the road. As if that made him a safe bet.

'You know, darling, you never know. I could never let a strange man come to my house. I don't know how you can do these things.'

'I know. You're right, I shouldn't,' I said. 'I don't usually do that.' And that was true: I don't. But I tried to explain that, for some reason, I just felt safe with him.

Except I really couldn't explain it. I knew that even normal-seeming trader-type guys could turn out to be nutcases. But in my many years of fucking around, I'd always been lucky. I may have had bad radar when it came to boyfriends like Karume, but I had good radar when it came to sex partners. I told Nadia I had liked Dr Donny's voice and that he had sounded smart and sexy and fun.

'Darling . . .'

'Anyway, he had an enormous cock. And he lives down the road and he's a hedge-fund trader. And now he's invited me to Monaco.'

'Are you going?'

I explained that I had to rearrange a few things first and that then I would let him know. But in my head, I'd already decided.

I waited a few hours before texting my answer, so as not to appear too keen.

I didn't hear back from Donny until after the weekend, when he popped up on Messenger.

'sorry i didnt get back to u but work got mental'

I deleted him from my phonebook and blocked his name on Messenger.

I felt let down – annoyed at having been conned, hurt at having been so quickly discarded, and surprised at having been so easily hooked. I don't mind the fuck-and-gos; in fact, I quite like them. If Donny hadn't suggested meeting up again, that would have been OK. But I do mind being lied to. It is totally unnecessary. We'd both got what we'd wanted. I didn't need a second thwarted fantasy on top of the first one that hadn't worked out quite as I'd imagined.

About a week later, whilst casually looking for playmates on Swinging Heaven, I stumbled across a new doctor ad.

'Have you a Doctor Fantasy?' it asked.

I pulled up the ad and saw Donny's pics. One of them was new: a head shot that was cropped right where a woman's head had once been. I figured it was his girlfriend or maybe a wife. Her long brown hair was still visible, spilling onto his shoulder.

> Hi Girls and Ladies
> Who gets turned on when they go and see their doctor?
> Well Dr Donny is here to fulfil those fantasises
> I'm a sex doctor who knows how to treat the symptons listed above.
> Would you like to have the hardest, longest and most satisfying cock you have ever had to relieve the stresses of your daily life ??
> Im totally clean, respectable, discreit and very st8.
> I live in London but can travel. Im available during the day sometimes as well.
> Get in touch soon and we can all have some fun.
> Ooops nearly forgot i promise to keep it a secret !!!!!
> Donny xxx

Perhaps I should have been flattered that Donny had taken inspiration from our morning tryst. But my first thought was that he'd nicked my fantasy. I sent him a message on Swinging Heaven pointing out his spelling mistakes.

Liar. Cad. Shitty speller. Still, I had to admit, I'd suck his cock again if the opportunity arose. It was beautiful.

2. MY SECRET

Dr Donny wasn't the first guy I'd had for breakfast, or rather, at meal times.

For about three years, I used my lunch hour for things other than eating lunch.

If you enjoy sex, and you've got a busy job and two growing and very nosy sons, then you have to work to slot in a session. I've always been resourceful when it comes to finding sex slots and, following my divorce, I had to be. It's not easy juggling a full-time job and the second full-time job of single parenthood. Some women like shopping in their off-time; I like sex. It makes me feel beautiful, it keeps me healthy, it's fun and it's free.

My noontime destination had been Rio's, a naturist spa not far from my office, where, after a quick steam and sauna, I would scout the premises until I found a man I wanted to fuck. Factoring in flirting time, a.k.a. foreplay, normally I could get laid and wash my hair and be out of there in under two hours.

But then my workload increased and suddenly I found I had no time for a sandwich, much less sex. Plus my receptionist caught on to my lunch-time gig, since I frequently arrived back at work with suspiciously wet hair. No longer feeling free to leave the office for long 'meetings', I came up with the idea of the breakfast break.

Sam was the inspiration for this idea.

Like most of the men in my mobile, I met Sam online after putting an ad on Swinging Heaven. One of my regulars decided to get serious with another woman, creating a vacancy on my dance card. By necessity, I turned to my handy website. Some women pine for one serious boyfriend; I prefer a half-dozen regulars. That way, I never go without. Guys in their late thirties and forties (my preferred age group) are extraordinarily busy. But when you have six men on speed dial, one is always available when another drops out.

As usual, in my subject header I put the three initials that mean the most to me: VWE. That's short for very well endowed.

The next day I scoured through the one hundred or so responses I received until one caught my eye. Presumably all the men who replied were VWE, as requested, but few got right to the point. Sam did. I liked that. When one is on the lookout for a regular fuck-buddy, brevity works best. Too many men write three-page emails telling exactly what they'll do if given the chance to meet me. They never will. Just as the Hollywood exec wants a movie synopsis that can be summed up in thirty seconds, I want a prospective date who can sell himself in thirty words. That shows intelligence – they're smart enough to have figured out the demands of the sexual marketplace – and it bodes well, because in addition to my big-cock fetish, I can't meet a man with whom I can't hold a conversation.

Sam told me his age, location, and cock size. Well, he didn't give a measurement, exactly, but noted that he was VVWE. That extra 'V' was all the information I needed. Finally, a man who understood exactly what's required.

I pulled up his pic. It showed a black man in tight white briefs, with big shoulders, pronounced abs and muscular thighs. He had one hand around a long hard cock, which protruded about five inches above the waistband of his briefs. VVWE indeed.

'You're cute,' I wrote. 'Free on Friday night?'

He was.

We arranged to meet at a wine bar just up the road from my house and, rare for such first meetings, Sam turned up on time.

He was shorter than I'd expected – about my height, five feet six inches – but looked exactly like his photo: fit, muscular, handsome. He had a squarish face and angular features. He wore jeans and a pale-blue polo shirt under a heavy leather jacket. He kissed me on one cheek, then took off his woollen hat and exposed his closely shaven head. He smiled warmly.

We ordered a bottle of Chardonnay and, as an icebreaker, I asked him whether he'd had any strange experiences on Swinging Heaven.

'Who hasn't?' he laughed. His accent was middle class, London inflected, educated.

'OK, you first,' I said.

'Which one do you want first?' he said. 'I have quite a few.'

'Your most extreme,' I said.

'Well, I was once asked over by a guy who wanted to watch while I fucked his wife,' he began.

'Oh, yeah,' I said, 'I know lots of guys who are used as thirds. They could make a living out of servicing the wives of married men. While the married man watches, or films, or participates.'

I wasn't expecting what followed, though.

'This guy didn't participate; he just coached.' Sam rolled his eyes. 'He didn't want me to use a condom – he insisted on that bit – and then, as I'm fucking his wife, he's standing at the foot of the bed directing me: *fuck her, fuck her harder, I want to see you come inside her*. The guy was pretty annoying. It was so distracting I had a hard time keeping it up. I'm actually more of a one-on-one-type guy.'

'I know what you mean,' I said. 'I hate too much talking during sex. Drives me mad.'

'Yeah,' he agreed, then continued with his story. 'Finally I come, shoot my load inside her. She gets up, sits on her husband's face – he's on the bed now, right? – and pushes my spunk out. Which he sucks out and swallows.'

'Gross,' I said, and laughed, suddenly feeling like an amateur. 'Gee, I just want you to fuck me. But I'll sit on your face if you want me to.'

'You are a gracious hostess,' he said, laughing and exposing beautiful, straight white teeth.

'And I'm well endowed – I have a big hot tub,' I said.

'Are you crazy? It's January. Isn't it a bit cold to be sitting outside in a pool of water?'

'Not when the water's thirty-eight degrees,' I said.

'OK, let's go,' he said. 'As long as you're talking Celsius and not Fahrenheit. You're American, right?'

We finished our wine as I explained how I'd moved to London at the age of thirteen but that, as he'd obviously noticed, my accent betrayed my roots.

'For someone who's been here that long, I'm surprised you still sound like a Yank,' he said. 'I'm sure I'm not the first person to tell you that.'

He wasn't. 'That's because it works,' I said. 'I haven't met a guy yet who doesn't like hearing a New York broad say, "I really wanna suck your cock." '

'You have a point,' he said. 'That does sound good.'

'Feels even better,' I said, laughing. 'Let's go.'

I slung on my sheepskin coat and three minutes later we were at my front door.

It was very cold that night. Sam took off his leather jacket and hung it on the banister, then went into the kitchen while I went upstairs to get some towels. I came back in time to see him remove his nut huggers. Even soft, his cock hung a good seven inches down his leg. And his body was even better than it appeared in the picture: leaner, fitter, tighter.

We ran straight to the hot tub in my back garden. Climbing into the steaming pool, we sat next to each other and let the water warm us and the jets massage our backs. I slid next to him, then probed under the surface and found his cock to be hard. It felt even bigger than it looked online.

'Not very private, is it?' said Sam, looking around, pretending not to notice what was going on underneath the water.

'No, not especially,' I had to admit. I counted the number of windows that overlooked the tub. Thirteen chances of getting an ASBO.

'Have your neighbours ever said anything? I assume I'm not the first guy in here.' He smirked, looking at me out of the corner of his eye.

'Oh, they're all far too polite,' I said. 'You know the English.'

I'd never found the idea of being watched a turn-on, but I'd never particularly minded it, either. If I wanted to have sex with someone, provided there weren't more than ten pervy guys around, I'd strip off and get down to it. I had a postage stamp of a garden, so it was a natural consequence that neighbours might spy on me. I was reconciled to that fact. Even so, I rarely ventured out to the tub before it was dark.

Presumably reassured, Sam moved closer to me and moved his fingers up my leg until he was fingering my clit. 'I really want to eat your pussy.'

'I really want you to eat my pussy,' I said. 'And fuck me up the ass.' I raised myself out of the water and, though freezing, sat on the edge of the tub, exposing my sex to him.

He leaned over and stuck his tongue between my legs, gently probing my clit.

That's the great thing about Swinging Heaven – you always

get guys who know what to do. They've had lots and lots of sex, and they know what they like. Practice does make perfect.

I moaned quietly as Sam lapped me up. 'Mmmm, that feels so good.'

After a few minutes, once the water on my wet body began to feel like icicles, I said, 'As good as that feels, I'm absolutely fucking freezing. And I really want to suck your cock.'

'What's stopping you? Certainly not the neighbours.'

Not the cold, either. We switched positions. Gratefully, I returned to the hot water, and Sam stood up, holding his huge cock out for me with one hand.

It was about 11 p.m. and pitch black outside. The moon cast light on the steam rising off his penis.

Lifting my body as little as possible out of the warm water, I caressed the tip of his cock with my tongue. I held the shaft with my right hand and massaged the sac with my left. I felt him grow longer and thicker in my mouth. I slid his cock further down my throat, easing the passage open to try to accommodate him. I couldn't.

Within just seconds his cock had grown too large to handle. 'I think we should go to my bedroom soon,' I said. I figured my pussy could handle him better than my mouth, and fucking would be a lot easier, and warmer, on the bed.

We jumped out of the tub and, laughing, ran in the freezing air towards the house. Our wet bodies were enveloped in steam. I looked at Sam. He was an apparition, almost out of focus and ghostlike under the eerie vapours.

No sooner had we entered the kitchen than he had me pinned. I had cheekily climbed onto the kitchen table, laid on my back and spread my legs, saying, 'I think the bedroom can wait,' and he concurred.

He slid his still-hard cock inside me, grabbing my bent legs underneath my knees and pulling me towards his chest. Though I have a very deep pussy, Sam's cock found the far end of it – but too soon.

'That's too deep,' I said, as he thrust repeatedly into me. 'Too fast. Slow down.' After just a minute it had become slightly painful. Fucking a monster cock might look great in porn movies, but in real life it's not always so pleasurable, at least not right away. I don't think any man had ever filled me up quite as much as Sam did. Accommodating him would take some getting used to.

'Sorry,' he said. 'I guess I got a bit carried away. Turn around.'

I climbed off the table and leaned over it. Normally I don't go for short guys. But after meeting Sam, I began to see the advantages of being with someone my own height. No matter what position we were in, his cock was at exactly the right place. I didn't have to crouch or stand on my toes for him to enter my pussy from behind.

The table wasn't particularly comfortable, but the idea of sex on top of it was hot. Feeling Sam sliding in and out of me was hotter still. As was the way he dominated me. Like many women, I enjoy being taken and told what to do. Perhaps the thinking behind it is a cliché but, having to boss people around at work, I don't want to have to do the same thing in bed.

Eventually we made it to the bedroom and we fucked for five hours, until Sam, a real gent, made me come first. He held back his own orgasm until the end of the night, when he finished inside my mouth.

'That was amazing,' he said. 'We must do that again.' And unlike Dr Donny, he really meant it.

I was game, but as we compared schedules we realised nights were out for us. I had my kids for all but two weekends a month. Sam was a care worker and spent many weeknights going to local community meetings. 'I don't start work till ten,' Sam said, as he got ready to leave. 'Maybe we can meet for breakfast sometime.'

I found the idea appealing. But at that moment, so was the idea of my bed. It was 4 a.m. when he walked out the door and 4:01 when I fell asleep.

I waited a couple of weeks before shooting Sam a text.

'What are you doing tomorrow morning at 9?' I tapped into my phone.

His response came back immediately: 'Fucking you.'

And he did. This time we went straight to the bedroom where, after juicing me up with his tongue, he rolled on a condom and then slid his thickness into my ass. I'd grown to love anal after living with Daniel for two years. He had slept with so many women, that the pussy no longer held any fascination for him. Anal was naughtier, he felt, and since he was very good at making sure it never hurt, I was happy to oblige. I learned from Daniel that the trick was to take it on my terms, in my own time, guiding the cock into my ass slowly as the muscles relaxed. Deep breathing helped too, filling my lungs with oxygen as Daniel's cock pushed in deeper. By the end of that relationship, I had become something of an anal expert and found it as horny as Daniel did.

Massaging my clit with a vibrator, I came as Sam gently entered and exited, slowly and rhythmically. After I came, Sam slipped me onto my back and massaged my clit whilst jerking himself off with his free hand. As per our first date, he came in my mouth.

'That was lovely,' I said afterwards, realising those were my first words since he'd arrived.

'You're telling me. Gotta run.'

'See you soon.'

We kissed and were both out the door within 45 minutes.

After that second meeting, we got together regularly, usually every other Friday, and soon developed a routine. I would drop my kids off at their school and get back home by nine. Sam would arrive promptly five minutes later, and then, after not much more than a hello, get busy. He'd fuck me until I came, come in my mouth, and be gone by 9.45.

I thought it was the perfect arrangement and it worked for Sam, too. In fact, he seemed to thrive on the time constraint. Knowing he had just a brief window of time made him focused. He wanted to get me off; for Sam, those mornings were all about me and my pleasure and in taking the fantasy to the next level, one step at a time. It was pleasurable because he understood my body and could get me to orgasm quickly. There aren't many men who are able to do that.

The only other man I'd ever been with who thrived on eleventh-hour sex was Frank, a long-distance boyfriend I dated around the time my marriage was coming to an end. A French-Irish guy from New York City, he had never been outside the US, so when he came to visit me one week, I took him to Woodstock, a traditional old English village near Oxford, for a few days of sex and sightseeing. Just before checkout, while packing my bag, I announced that we had to be out of the room in ten minutes. The bed was covered with suitcases and clothing and guidebooks, but that didn't prevent him from pushing me down on the mattress and climbing on top of me. He lifted up my skirt and entered me without any foreplay, and came three minutes later. I didn't come, but that hardly mattered; he had made me come numerous times during his visit. We were at the front desk by deadline.

Ordinarily he was a guy who really liked to take his time, and it was not unusual that a session with Frank lasted four hours – thus my willingness to carry on with the relationship despite the three thousand miles between us. But that ten-minute window in Woodstock had pushed a button I'd never known existed. I should have caught on earlier. He told me once that he'd gone through a period during his thirties of being with hookers. That's a habit that comes with expensive time constraints, and I think Frank liked the idea of having to get off to the clock.

I didn't think Sam was into prostitutes, but he certainly liked his 45-minute quickie, and so did I. It was the only chance I got to get laid outside of my designated two kids-free weekends a month. Following the end of my disastrous relationship with Karume, my last serious boyfriend, I'd made a pact with myself never to invite another man over during the week when my kids were around, unless I felt there was a chance of a serious relationship. Sam was not serious – just serious fun – so I didn't feel I was breaking my rule, especially as my kids never met him.

I was still feeling the woozie post-sex glow as I walked through my office door.

'Good morning,' I said to my receptionist, a busty blonde cutie in her late twenties.

She smiled as she greeted me, as she always did. It seemed just another day at work for her, but as I walked towards my office, I laughed to myself, remembering my horny breakfast.

Sam was my secret, and it was a turn-on going into the office, having been royally fucked, and being the only person who knew.

I realised that day I wasn't the only one with a secret.

'I have something to tell you that I haven't told anyone else,' said the voice at the end of my phone. 'Can we have lunch?' It was James, a colleague who worked in television advertising.

I wondered what could be so important. He'd never really talked about his personal life before, although he enjoyed hearing, from time to time, about mine. I had met him a couple of years earlier when we worked on a project together professionally, and we grew close enough that eventually we got around to talking about sex. Or rather, I did. He was always evasive and fell into the role of eager listener.

James was in his late forties, married to a woman he had met at university, and the father of a couple of kids. He was bald, had glasses, and was of average height and weight and build – in fact, pretty much average in every way. Not unattractive, but not standout, either. Instead of 'sexy', he was the kind of guy who seemed safe and would be referred to as 'nice'. And he was.

We arranged to meet at a gastro pub near my office at one.

A family of six were sitting a few seats away from us, the children climbing on and off the chairs and making noise whilst the parents tried, unsuccessfully, to contain them. Two women and a man were quietly conducting business on our other side. We ordered roast pork sandwiches with crackling, a hearty meal that suited the crisp, wintry weather outside.

I took my cue from James, and played along as we caught up on business. Eventually he got around to the real reason for lunch.

'I haven't had sex in six years,' he said.

'Wow,' I said. 'That beats my four. Well, not four years since I've had sex, but you know what I mean.' He knew about the long spell without sex I endured towards the end of my marriage to David. Since then I'd been making up for lost time.

I suddenly wondered if James was one of those guys who wanked on cam – solitary, feverish, and eager for any sexual connection, going cyber when there was nothing real on offer. Not that I hadn't been online myself. But it was always as an adjunct to a busy, and varied, sex life. Yet I often suspected that many of the men jerking on cam were in front of their computer because they weren't getting any in bed and it was their only form of relief.

'I haven't told anybody else,' continued James. 'You're the only person I can talk to.'

I felt sad. We hardly knew each other, and it was heartbreaking knowing he couldn't confide in his mates. His whole forties were a desert. No wonder he hangs out with me, I thought. It hadn't occurred to me that James had probably lived vicariously through my sex stories. Or that they might have pained him. Over my six years of singledom I'd met at least a dozen men just like James who wouldn't leave home to find a satisfying life for fear of having their kids taken from them.

'Have you and your wife talked about this?' I asked.

'Well, that's the thing,' he said. 'I had a chat with her a while back and told her that I really missed having sex. She told me it's not that she doesn't love me, but she's not interested. She just doesn't feel any sexual desire.'

'That's not uncommon,' I said. 'I felt that way, too, when I was married.' I explained that it wasn't my husband's fault, but rather the stress of bringing up kids and being tired all the time and just not feeling sexy. 'It's hard to feel sexy when there's baby spittle all over your clothes.'

'I can understand that,' said James, 'but our kids aren't babies any more. And I really want to get laid.'

Suddenly, I began to wonder if he had invited me to lunch to help him out. I had encountered other men who'd assumed that, because I was sexually active, they could have me. That had always pissed me off – the presumption that I wasn't choosy just because I liked getting laid.

I soon realised that wasn't the case with James. He just wanted to vent. He told me that he didn't want to move out on his wife and that he'd never cheated on her, but that he couldn't stand being celibate for much longer.

'Last week, I had drinks with one of my clients, a married woman,' he continued. 'One thing led to another, and she ended up giving me a blowjob in the car park.'

'I thought you said you never cheated.'

'Well,' he said, 'I'm still trying to work out the boundaries. I mean, we didn't sleep together. So it's not really cheating, is it?' It wasn't that he was looking for absolution; he really wasn't sure if he'd crossed the line.

'Oh,' I said, 'I think you'll find most people would say that getting sucked off in a car park is cheating. I think we can pretty much universally agree on that one. Sorry to disappoint you.'

James laughed.

'It must have been one amazing blowjob after a six-year hiatus.' I thought he'd laugh, but instead he suddenly looked glum.

'I tell you, I almost cried,' he said. 'I mean it. I was that close to crying.'

I didn't know what to say. How do you tell a man who hasn't had sex for six years that his marriage is dead? According to most of the men I've met over the years, a car park blowjob soon leads to a hotel room, and then to a pay-as-you-go mobile that allows you to schedule the next liaison. A year or two later, you've handed the house keys over to your wife and are sitting in a tiny apartment, the only thing you can afford after the alimony payments. But at least you're getting laid. I'd been there myself and had grown used to the financial insecurity. Still, it was a small price to pay for happiness.

I said the only thing I could. 'Maybe you should talk to your wife again. See if she's open to your having an arrangement whereby every once in a while you spend a night in London. It's not unheard of. You might be surprised at her reaction.'

'You're right,' he said. 'Maybe I should just be upfront with her.'

'And if that doesn't work,' I continued, 'you can always do what I do.' I told him about my virtual wanking. 'It's not really cheating if you're not in the same room.'

3. ANOTHER MAN, ANOTHER BLOWJOB

Thinking about James describing his car-park blowjob as a non-cheating event made me chuckle to myself. I felt bad that he was in a bind in his marriage, but I wasn't too worried about him. He had reconciled himself to the idea of getting sucked off in car parks and hotel rooms and God knows where else, either with the woman he'd just met or with the others who were sure to follow. Once you're back on the sex train, you don't make any stops.

I knew. I was celibate during the last four years of my marriage before meeting Frank from New York. He turned me on to swinging, fetish clubs, exhibitionism, anal, blowjobs, and good old-fashioned fucking again. After my affair with Frank, I realised all the fun I'd been missing during my relatively sex-free marriage, and I haven't stopped having fun since. I was confident that, on James's express route to future orgasms, now that he'd broken six years of celibacy, he'd be OK, all the while making excuses to his wife and justifying his behaviour, telling himself his affairs were inconsequential.

I'd figured out a long time ago that men have a gift for concocting excuses for their indiscretions and creating boundaries that suit their desires. My first boyfriend, Tim, from university, taught me this lesson one term after disappearing for three days. Eventually I tracked him down – in the apartment of a close girlfriend of mine. He wasn't wearing any trousers when I found him, but he assured me that he and Marsha were only friends. They moved in together within a couple of months and I cried my eyes out for a year after that. They remained together for a decade, and I got wise.

By the time I came across Mark, during one of my Friday evening sessions at Rio's, men and their twisted boundaries were water off this duck's back. For several years Rio's has been my home away from home, my refuge from Medialand and all its artifice. A naturist 'health club' in Kentish Town, it serves as a hook-up spot for men and women looking for a quickie, a threesome, or sometimes, on a lucky day, even a gang bang in one of the club's private rooms. It is frequented by all sorts, from government workers, property developers and video producers to lawyers, builders and security guards.

Even so, it is the one place I know where one's occupation is immaterial. Being naked means being free of dinner-party chat. I've often thought that the liberation from small talk is one of the reasons why I enjoy sex so much – when the clothes come off, so too does the bullshit that most guys carry around with them.

That Friday evening Rio's session began with me lying face down and naked in the steam room. I was pretending to be asleep, whilst half-hoping someone attractive might offer me a real massage, not just the cursory back rub as a prelude to fingering my pussy or bum, as was usually the case.

When I felt a damp towel spill onto my toes, I took exception to the clueless approach, so I ignored the towel and the person who came with it, and carried on lying immobile with my eyes closed. If I'm lucky, I thought, whoever dropped that towel on my toes will leave soon.

Next, I felt drops of warm water, like raindrops, on my back. Moisture from the ceiling, I hoped. I peeked from the corner of my eye and realised the damp towel had been dropped by the hairy Middle Eastern man I'd clocked on my way in, a quarter of an hour earlier. I ignored him – I don't do big hairy guys – but he persisted in trying to get my attention, finally addressing me after his effort failed to engage.

'I am professional masseur,' he said. 'You want back rub?'

I did not respond.

'Yes, professional masseur. I make you happy. Yes?'

I gave up. 'Where do you work, then?' I asked, keeping my eyes closed and my head turned towards the wall. I hoped I'd get a one-word answer and then be left alone.

'Yes, I'm professional masseur,' he repeated, as if that were his only line. Most men in Rio's had a whole inventory of them.

Either he hadn't heard my question or he didn't want to address it. It hardly mattered. He was about 45 and overweight and had a moustache. But it was the hair springing out of every pore, particularly on his back and shoulders, that killed it for me. I was not averse to a massage from a stranger, but I wasn't desperate. Besides, I'd set aside the time for relaxation and had only just arrived. A massage could wait. For now, I wanted to lie in the steam room and bide my time, waiting for a more perfect male specimen to show up. Or maybe I'd just fall asleep. I continued to lie on the bench, content to ignore the masseur and everyone else in the room.

The drops splashing on my back continued, then suddenly became more frequent. Ten minutes later, I opened my eyes and sat up, wrapping the towel I'd been lying on around my waist. The room was filled with steam, but I could just make out three figures standing in front of me, having sex. A Latin-looking transvestite was sandwiched between two men: the Middle Eastern masseur and another figure, indistinct in the steam. I realised that the raindrops I'd assumed were coming off the steam-room ceiling were in fact a spray of sweat dripping off the threesome's bodies.

It wasn't the first time I'd witnessed a threesome in the steam room, but in the past it had always involved me. A few years earlier I'd been the centre of one particularly steamy session. It hadn't lasted long because the room was so hot; the sweat caused one man's condom to keep slipping off, and the other couldn't stay hard. I liked the idea of our sweaty threesome, and the way our wet bodies fell all over each other, but I came to the conclusion that steam-room sex works best in the movies.

I left the steam room and moved to the Jacuzzi. Here, the view was better. I spotted a handsome Irishman I'd met once before. He was in his late thirties, about six-feet tall and very slim. He had fair hair, blue eyes, wide cheekbones and big white teeth – typically Irish, right down to the tattoos: a Celtic band that wrapped around one upper arm and a Celtic cross that decorated his lower back.

I hadn't seen him for two years, when I'd had to break up a near fight between him and another guy. I was in the shower, the Irish guy was in the shower next to me, and a stranger with a hard-on hovered between us, ogling. Mr Ireland had taken offence, thinking the erection was for his benefit.

He hadn't aged since that day; he'd just changed his hair a bit – it was now shorter and spiked on top.

Mr Ireland was alone in one of the Jacuzzi. I removed my towel, hung it on a peg, and stepped into the warm water. 'Haven't seen you here for a while,' I said.

'And you,' he said with a faint accent. He was grinning.

'Last time I saw you, I broke up a fight between you and some guy with a hard-on.'

'Yes, I remember that day,' he said. 'He's here today, actually. I've seen him here quite a few times since then. He even says hello to me from time to time.'

I felt his hand touch my breast under the water. I pretended not to notice. It was more fun that way. We'd not had sex before, but I remembered seeing him in the shower that previous time, and now I wanted it.

'That's what I like about Rio's,' I said. 'You make the strangest kinds of friendships'.

He explored my nipples as we carried on talking. 'I'm enjoying playing with your nipples,' he said, finally.

'Yes, I noticed.'

'I hope you don't mind.'

'I don't mind,' I said playfully.

We sat in the Jacuzzi for a few minutes more, talking. He played with my tits. I reached for his cock. It was hard. It was long.

'You wouldn't like to go upstairs, would you?' he asked.

'Sure,' I said.

'I'll meet you in the lounge in a minute. I have to wait to get out of the Jacuzzi, if you know what I mean.'

I knew what he meant. I laughed and wondered how long his hard-on would take to subside and why he'd want to bother, as he was going to have to get it up again. I felt energised knowing that he wanted to be with me.

I stepped out of the Jacuzzi, grabbed my towel, and walked into the lounge. I stood at the edge of the room, so as not to attract anyone's attention, and looked at the TV fixed to the wall. It was showing the horse races at Sandown.

Five minutes later, my Irishman came up to me and together we walked towards the door that led upstairs.

He led me to the room at the end of the hall. 'This is the biggest room,' he said. 'Door open or closed? I don't mind, either way.'

'Door closed,' I said. 'I don't feel like putting on a show today.' I wanted him all to myself. Since seeing him that first time two years earlier, I'd wanted him. I'd even looked for him after that, and now he was mine. At least for the next thirty minutes.

'Door closed it is, then,' he said.

I sat down on the edge of the platform. It was low enough that, while sitting, my head was at cock height. He removed his towel as I took his cock in my mouth. He had a semi, already about five inches long.

Bending over, he reached for my nipples and rubbed circles around them with his index fingers as he grew harder. My mouth took him further in. But with this guy, it wasn't about size, I just found him really sexy. There was a natural chemistry between us. I liked his voice, his chilled attitude, the way he touched me.

I continued sucking his cock for another minute or so, and then he said, 'I can't have full sex.'

I looked up.

'I hope you don't mind,' he added.

I did mind. I had assumed we were in a couple's room for a bit more coupling. I could have blown him in the Jacuzzi or the steam room. But I wasn't about to argue with a cock in my mouth. Even though I was disappointed, I continued sucking.

'May I come in your mouth?' he asked a few minutes later.

I nodded.

Within seconds I felt the warm liquid in my mouth and I swallowed. I continued to suck gently, until I felt his cock go soft.

I sat up, reached my arms around his shoulders and drew him to me. I kissed him on the lips.

'I was so horny,' he said. 'I really needed that.'

'Always happy to oblige,' I said. 'I only came here for a bloody back rub, but that was almost as good.'

'I'll rub your back, if you'd like,' he offered.

'Would you? That would be great. My shoulders are a mess.' Hunching over a computer all week left me feeling tense and stiff. That's why Rio's, which tries to sell itself as a health club, though its members all knew better, really does serve as one for me from time to time.

Ten minutes later my Irishman had pummelled out my knots, even cracked my upper spine with a couple of quick twists of my neck.

'That was great,' I said. 'Are you a chiropractor?'

'I'm a builder,' he said. That explained the tone of his muscles.

'And a hunk. What's your name, anyway?'

'Mark.'

'Suzanne. Nice to meet you, officially.'

He smiled as we walked downstairs together. I showered, then looked for Mark in the changing room to wave goodbye. I mounted my bicycle, which was chained to a lamppost outside, and rode home, smiling.

I walked into my loft, turned on the PC, and signed on to Messenger. Scott was online.

I'd first contacted Scott through Nerve.com. I hadn't been on the site for over a year, but had been a regular on and off since 2000. It was a sentimental favourite, as that's where I'd met Frank, the New Yorker with whom I had the affair that both recharged my sex batteries and led to my divorce. The site had been free in its early days, so it had been easy to make contact with guys. After Nerve started charging, I moved on to cheaper pastures. Then I received an email telling me I'd been allocated 2,000 points – the equivalent of a cash balance, with deductions made for every wink and message – after Nerve settled a lawsuit with another website. I had no idea what their legal mess was about, but I was happy to have a subsidised look around again. That's when I found Scott.

He was a tall, slim, blue-eyed divorced American guy based in the UK. My type.

'I just got 2,000 points and have decided to use them on you,' I wrote him.

'Gee, I'm flattered,' he wrote back. 'I'm travelling at the mo. Back end month.' He gave me his personal email address and suggested we meet up when he returned.

That had been twelve months earlier. I'd given up on Scott, although every month or so we'd have an online chat. I quickly discovered that Scott's job with a global news syndicator required that he spend more time in the air than on the ground. So, despite a few emails back and forth and some chats over MSN, we never found a date when we could get together.

'So, where are you this time?' I wrote one day, checking in.

'In London.'

'How long?'

'Quick stop. Leaving on Sunday.'

It seemed too good to be true and, suddenly realising that my dance card was empty, I made a snap decision. 'Want to meet up tomorrow?'

'Sure,' he said. 'Just make sure it's a rooftop.'

I didn't ask why, but the only rooftop I knew was at my other home away from home, after Rio's – Soho House. We arranged to meet on the roof terrace the next day.

Over dinner he told me about his job, pointedly noting that although it involved nearly nonstop travel around the globe, it brought in piles of money. He was a braggart, but I liked him anyway. His travelling stories were funny and he had a wry sense of humour. And he was cute, especially after a few bottles of Sancerre, which he kept ordering at £55 a bottle.

He had a lived-in face and big sexy eyes and the kind of runner's build I'd always found attractive. As I looked across the table at him, I hoped he found me as sexy as I found him.

'Let's go back to mine and sit in my hot tub.'

He agreed, and a few minutes later we were out the door.

As we stepped out of the club, Scott pulled me close.

'Stop. I have to kiss you.' Pinning me against the wall of the building, he stooped over me, his six-foot-four frame practically bent over double to reach my lips.

He slipped his tongue in my mouth and then breathed down my throat.

So much for being friends, I thought.

We walked hand in hand down the street.

'We'll pick up a bottle of wine on the way back,' he said.

'I've got wine at home. We're fine.'

'I'm an alpha male, Suzanne. I'll buy the wine. That's the way it is.'

I laughed. It sounded like a line out of a movie. An alpha male. Who did he think he was, Rambo? Yet, there were some benefits to the machismo. I thought about my overdraft and was glad Rambo had picked up the bill.

'I just want us to be *friends*,' he'd said over the first bottle of Sancerre. Now he was beginning to sound like Mark, the sexy Irishman from Rios who'd massage but not fuck me. I wondered whether this was going to turn into a weekend of abstinence, something I hadn't counted on with either guy.

That disappointed me, but that's the way it goes sometimes. OK, I thought, I'll run with that one … for now.

I hoped, as I stared into his blue eyes and shared bottle after bottle, that Scott might come around. And the drunker I got, the more I liked the idea of our being friends, particularly if it were on my terms – friends with benefits. Most of the men I met were short dates or quick fucks; good lays, not buddies. We didn't ring each other to chat; we rang to make a date. Scott, however, was a guy I could envision having a chinwag with.

Even if fucking wasn't on the menu, I expected it would be good if it happened. In my experience, it's almost impossible to find a guy who is smart and funny and not good in bed. But sex wasn't Scott's main attraction; it was the laughter and the shared background that got me. And I could tell Scott needed a pal, too. If I got a friend who occasionally climbed into my bed after a night of big laughs and good food and fun times, it was a win-win.

I fancied some real intimacy for a change, not just a few hours straight out of a porn flick. Despite the fact that he was well travelled, I got the impression Scott didn't sleep around. 'Lots of women come on to me,' he said. 'But I'm not really a one-nighter kind of guy. I'd really just like having friends. I'm actually quite lonely. Aren't you?'

'Not really, no.' That was true. I had plenty of pals. Even so, I thought it would be fun to have one who was a fellow American.

Then Scott said something that I hadn't heard for a while. 'The thing is, I'm really feeling a connection here. Aren't you?'

Just as I like variety in my sex partners, I like variety in my relationships with guys. I want good ol' vanilla mixed up with a bit of domination, followed by cuddling – a bit o' this 'n' a bit o' that. Now I was thinking no-sex/yes-sex/lonely-horny Scott might want a bit of a mix himself.

It was nice spending time with a fellow American. We shared the same cultural history, knew the same stupid TV shows. Talking with Scott was like having a reunion with a hometown acquaintance. I began to think he had the makings of a fun, regular playmate, a trade-up from a one-night shag. Somehow, his masculine arrogance was more turn-on than off-putting.

'I have hundreds of people who want to do exactly what I tell them to do, who *have* to do exactly what I tell them to do,' he said when the subject of Scott came round as it often did. 'I mean, there are people who think my word is the gospel. They call it Scott's World.' He laughed. I wasn't sure if I should. 'In India, where I do a lot of business,' he continued, 'people say that you're all right if you're in Scott's World.'

I understood being a boss with her own desk, her own office. I'd never met a person who thought he ruled the world and then named it after himself.

'How much money do you make?' he asked, somewhat to my surprise even though the question seemed true to his brash character.

I told him.

'Is that all?'

'Yes, that's all,' I said, surprised again, given that it was many times the average UK salary.

'I make a lot more than that,' he said.

'But does it make you happy?'

'It's who I am.'

'That wasn't what I asked.'

He looked at me, confused. 'It's who I am.'

Then he took out his wallet and showed me a picture of his daughter. Although just seven, she looked like him, with sandy-blonde hair, high cheekbones and a wide smile.

'She's gorgeous,' I said.

'She's more important to me than anyone else in the world,' Scott said. Unfortunately, he only got to see her every couple of weeks and then only for a day or two, until he was back on a jet. I tried to fit together what he had told me over our dinner date: that money drove him, that he was the master of his domain, that he adored his little girl but rarely found the time to see her. It seemed kind of sad.

I looked across the table at him. I noticed the wrinkles at the corner of his eyes, the dark circles underneath, the tight dry skin that seemed starved of moisture and oxygen. He looked exhausted. The message on his face said, 'I need to sleep for a week.'

Scott chain-smoked through dinner, taking three or four puffs on a cigarette, then putting it out and lighting another. He was kind of a mess. Yet, I kept thinking there was something attractive about him that I couldn't put my finger on.

I don't like smokers, won't even date one after having lived with one for two years and almost gone mad. But then, I rationalised, I wasn't looking for a live-in. I could put up with the cigarettes for the occasional overnight.

Despite all his bravado, I got the sense Scott needed someone. I saw myself becoming his confidante, maybe even his friend. It was so rare that I met an American in London, and I liked the idea of having a fellow ex-pat buddy. Especially since his irreverent monologues made me laugh.

'The other day,' he told me, 'I was giving a lecture to three hundred people in New Delhi. The Indians wouldn't stop bobbing their heads. So, I told them, "If you don't mind, can you stop bobbing your heads up and down, because I'm finding it very distracting." '

I'd been to India a couple of times myself and could picture the head-bobbing to which he referred. It was as much a part of being Indian as rubbing noses was for Eskimos. I tried to imagine Scott telling people to stop a habit that was so culturally ingrained.

'But that's the way Indians are,' I said.

'Yes, I know. But it was really putting me off my speech.'

Arrogant and self-centred and culturally insensitive he was indeed, but I wanted to take him home anyway. I wanted to sit this manic man in my hot tub and help him relax. I wanted him to escape from Scott's world and take a break in my world.

After Mark and the one-sided oral, the other thing I wanted was some action of my own.

We jumped in a cab and were back at my house within the hour. We immediately undressed and got in the hot tub. Straight away, Scott's lips found mine. I moved closer and straddled him. I felt his hard-on pressing against my pussy. I kissed him again, rubbing my pussy against him, teasing his shaft with my labia, sliding myself up and down it.

'You know, I'm pretty toasted,' Scott said as he reached for the bottle of wine he'd insisted on buying and which I'd put on a shelf by the tub. 'And I have to be up early. I should go.'

'Why don't you stay,' I said. 'It's silly to get a cab back now. I promise I'll wake you up in the morning with a cup of hot coffee.'

It didn't take much to convince him.

As soon as we fell into bed, Scott began kissing me and reaching towards my pussy. His long fingers probed inside me. Then he moved down the bed and put his head between my legs and began to eat me out. His tongue was insistent and confident. I moaned with delight, and moved my legs onto his shoulders, spreading my legs apart.

Scott put his fingers inside me while his tongue continued its exploration of my clit.

'Turn over,' he said.

I did as instructed. Then he told me to get on all fours. Thinking that he might fuck me from behind, I opened the bedside drawer containing my sex toys and condoms. I pulled out some anal beads and a condom.

'These look interesting,' he said, picking up the anal beads.

'Yes, they're a favourite of mine. Wanna have a go?' I said.

Scott was intrigued. Gradually he pushed all twelve inches of the toy up my bottom, leaving just the ring at the end hanging out of my ass. His fingers continued to work my pussy. I felt myself opening up to him. First one finger went in, then a second. Each addition made me wetter. Scott was a lot naughtier than I'd expected him to be, and he was dominant. I'm liking Scott's World, I thought.

'Open up to me,' he said.

He inserted a third finger. I felt my pussy give way. It felt like his whole hand was inside me, working its way up and down my pussy. It felt so good I screamed, so loudly I thought I might wake up the newborn baby next door.

'What else do you have in that drawer?' Scott asked when I calmed down.

'There's a strap-on . . .'

'Really?' he said. 'Ever use it?'

'Sure, a couple of times. Want to try it?'

'That might be interesting,' he said. 'I've never been fucked before.'

I thought that for a straight guy, he wasn't acting so straight. I'd only met two guys in my life who'd gone for strap-on action.

I buckled the strap-on around my waist. Instantly, it gave me a sense of power and control. So much for being an alpha male, I thought as I started lubing Scott's ass and telling him what to do.

'Get on all fours,' I said.

He got on his knees, but I could see his height was going to be a problem. I couldn't reach his anus.

'Sorry,' I said. 'That's not going to work. Try getting on your back and lifting your legs. You're too tall for me.'

He turned over and put his long legs in the air. I squatted down and aimed the tip of the dildo at his ass, slowly trying to ease it in the hole. It was not the most comfortable position.

'Go on, baby,' I said. 'Give it up to me. I'm going to fuck you.' I tried to sound authoritative, dominant, even if it came out forced. 'Come on,' I continued. 'Open up.' I pushed the dildo in a little more. 'I'm going to fuck you real good.'

I pushed in a little farther. Part of me enjoyed the domination, but the other part felt it wasn't really my character.

But Scott moaned, so it seemed to be working.

Squatting down more, I carried on pushing and talking like a top. 'I'm going to fuck your ass. Give it up for me.'

I gave one more thrust and Scott screamed. He shot up on the bed. 'Fuck!' he said. 'That really hurt. I mean *really* hurt.'

That brought me back to earth. 'I'm so sorry, Scott. I didn't mean to hurt you. I guess the position was really awkward. You're so big, it's hard to find the right position, you know?'

'I'm never going to do *that* again. Fuck!'

After a few minutes his pain subsided. Then, apparently back to normal, Scott began to wank. Five minutes later, he came all over my face.

Drunk and exhausted, we went to sleep. Or tried to. Shortly after Scott rolled over to one side of the bed, his breathing changed and I knew he was asleep. I knew, because Scott became a noise machine. It wasn't gentle snoozing, but snoring and grunting and sniffling. That'll teach me, I thought. I hadn't been with a sleep-killer since my partner Daniel had died three years earlier, and I'd forgotten what a price it was to pay for company in the bedroom.

After falling in and out of sleep for hours, I tried breathing to Scott's rhythm, but soon realised I was putting more effort into matching the ever-changing rhythm than into trying to fall back to sleep. First, there was the heavy gasping for breath, followed by a few snorts. Then came the trombone honks from his nose, then the gurgling of his throat. Then blessed silence. A minute later, the pattern repeated. Gasp, snort, honk, gurgle. Silence. Gasp, snort, honk, gurgle. Silence.

I was really tired. I was also really drunk. I knew sleep would not have come easy even in the best circumstances. It never did when I'd had more than two glasses of wine. And Scott and I had shared almost four bottles. That'll teach me, I thought, again.

I got out of bed and quietly opened the bedside cabinet, hoping to find the wax earplugs I used to wear when Daniel snored beside me. I found my butt plug, a selection of vibrators and a blindfold, but couldn't find the earplugs. I contemplated turning on the light to have a better look around, but remembering that Scott had to wake up early, I didn't want to disturb him. So I made the best of it: I wrapped myself around Scott's body.

There was a lot to wrap around: his torso was long and broad, his slim legs went on for miles, his tight bum was a hill of meaty flesh. The sound effects were excruciating, but at least if I were going to lie awake, I had a delightful body to cling to.

A few hours later, I woke Scott with the promised cup of coffee. Then, noticing his morning hard-on, I took the initiative and straddled one of his legs.

'Suck my cock, baby.'

I took him into my mouth.

God, he really gets me, I thought, as I leaned over to obey. No tedious discussion about what he was into, no distracting monologue telling me what he wanted to do to me and how and in what position, just a straightforward command. I had a swinging partner who rarely spoke during sex. When Greg, my regular, spoke it was only to tell me what he wanted me to do next. 'Lick my balls. Twist my nipples. Sit on my face.' That turned me on, and it spoiled me on the mattress-mouth types.

I spit onto the mushroom head, to lubricate the shaft for my sliding hand.

Scott grabbed the top of my head and pushed my mouth farther down his cock until I gagged.

'That's right, baby,' he repeated. 'Suck it good.'

I felt myself get wet and his cock get harder in my hands.

'Mmmn,' I moaned, more to myself than for his benefit. 'Mmmmmmmn.'

I felt him get harder as I continued riding his shaft. I removed my mouth and started wanking him furiously.

Scott stopped me. 'Not yet, baby. I'll tell you when I want to come.'

I loved being called 'baby'.

So, I slowed down, working my mouth around the head of his cock, my right hand working the shaft up and down.

'Cup my balls.'

I cupped his balls.

'Lick them.'

I licked, as ordered.

'Stroke me.'

I stroked.

'I'm going to come soon,' Scott said shortly afterwards. I felt his body begin to tremble and the pulsing of the veins that ran down the full length of his long hard cock.

'I'm coming, baby,' he said, panting. 'Take it.'

I felt his warm come drip down my throat. I continued sucking, but his cock was too sensitive.

'Ah!' he almost shouted. 'No!'

I pulled away from him. Between our attempts with the strap-on and now this post-orgasm sensitivity, it was clear I didn't know Scott's boundaries yet. But then, it's hard to know anything for certain after just one night with somebody. I took the obvious cue and left his cock alone.

I looked at the sheets. They were a MapQuest pattern of the route we'd taken the previous evening and that morning. All the evidence from an odd night and its morning after, there in friendly earth tones.

I still felt bad that I'd pushed too hard with the strap-on and that Scott had screamed with pain. I regretted being such a novice. Anal can be the ultimate pleasure with an experienced lover. But I was not an experienced top and Scott was not an experienced bottom, and I knew it was unlikely he would ever try anal again. There's nothing like having your anal cherry popped by an amateur to put you off the act. I knew that pain myself, having been taken there hundreds of times, and not always gently or by pros. It is easy for a top to get overexcited and push too hard before the bottom is ready, especially with a virgin ass. For all my experience in bed, I'd fucked-up sex like a bumbling newby.

If the plus to sleeping with lots of hot strangers is the excitement of a new body, a new cock, a new sexual adventure, the minus is that you don't know their limits. You can never be sure if you've read a new partner right or touched his body the way he really likes it touched. I didn't know if I'd be seeing Scott again and get the opportunity to know him, and his body and limits, the way I wanted to. Despite feeling a connection the night before, I feared we'd both pushed the boundaries for a first date.

I kissed Scott goodbye at the door, then walked back upstairs and pulled the sheets off the bed.

4. THE REUNION

I didn't hear from Scott after the strap-on incident, so figured I'd definitely blown it. But since I continued to feel weird about the pain I'd caused him, I shot him an email to clear the air.

'Hope all's well,' I wrote. 'Sorry if things got a little out of control that night.'

When I didn't hear back right away, I assumed we were history. Then, about a week later, a response was in my inbox.

'It was really great to meet you,' he wrote. 'You're right; it did get out of control. I hope that doesn't weird us both out and ruin what I think would be a very cool friendship.'

I was relieved and also pleased to think Scott might become, as I'd hoped that night we'd met, a friend with benefits. He said he was just about to embark on major travel again but suggested we stay in touch. 'Don't read silence as any sort of regret on my part,' he added.

Perhaps we'd have the opportunity to try again.

I made a mental note to use more lube next time around.

Till Scott came back to London, I thought I'd kill time with my regulars and go to my local, Rio's.

I hadn't been there in a while and, when I paid my £2 entry toll to the cutie American receptionist, I got a question in return. 'Can I ask you something?' he asked.

'Yes.'

'You know what I'm going to ask you, don't you?'

'Yes, I think I do.'

'It's you, isn't it?'

'Yes.' I smiled, arched an eyebrow. My cover was blown. They knew I was the one who'd written the erotic memoir that featured more than a few scenes in their sauna, Jacuzzi and couples' rooms. I wasn't sure I liked the staff knowing who I was, but now that they did, I kind of hoped they'd return the favour and give me a lifetime membership. After all, my book was practically an advertisement for Rio's.

'So, you're Suzanne.'

'Yes, I'm Suzanne.'

'We weren't sure,' he said. 'We've all been reading your book. A few of us thought it might be this other American woman that comes here. But I knew it was you.'

He looked proud of himself, as if he'd worked out an elaborate puzzle from the Gadget Shop.

'Guess I'm not so invisible any more. You won't tell anyone, will you?' I said. 'I'd rather everyone else didn't know.'

'Your secret is safe with me.'

That's good, I thought. I just wanted to go about my business. The business of getting laid.

I changed out of my clothes and walked over to the steam room. I was standing outside, debating whether to go in, when I saw Mark, Mr Ireland. I hadn't seen him in a few months.

Now, there he was, sitting on a green plastic garden chair, relaxing by the showers. I walked up to him.

'You wouldn't fancy giving me a back rub later on, would you?'

'Sure,' he said, looking up, smiling. 'Just give me a half-hour to chill out. Then I'll meet you outside the changing room.'

I killed some time in the sauna, then, once again, we were climbing the stairs together.

Since the last time I'd been in Rio's, the management had tacked plastic tubing filled with red lights around the doorways to each of the couples' rooms. It bathed the hallway in a trashy red glow. I'd always treated the private rooms as my personal bordellos, so I welcomed the change. It seemed appropriate.

'Who needs to go to Amsterdam, when we've got our own mini red light district in Kentish Town?' I said.

Mark laughed. We entered the largest room, which was at the far end of the hall across from the one where we'd had our first encounter.

I closed the door behind us, as Mark lay our towels down on the blue plastic mats that covered the platform. It was a familiar ritual.

As I turned to face him, he pulled me towards him. He put his arms around me and kissed me hard. His tongue was insistent. His body responded instantly. I felt his cock grow hard against my stomach but resisted the urge to touch it. I wanted to make him wait. It was a role-playing thing, more for my own benefit than his. I wanted to build the tension.

'I haven't had sex in weeks,' I said. 'I'm horny as hell.' Comments like that build anticipation. Most men get off on being the first, and if they're not the ones to pop your cherry, breaking a girl's abstinence is the next best thing. In this case, then the latter was true. I'd gone weeks without, been too busy even to call my usual fuck buddies. I was really glad I'd not had sex in so long, because I'd hoped to see Mark again, and here I was finally getting my wish.

'I haven't had it in *months*,' he replied. He grabbed my hands and held them above my head so I was pinned against the door. He kissed me again. It was more urgent this time. It wasn't desperation so much as need. He wanted me as badly as I wanted him.

I grabbed his bum to pull him into me and he moved one hand down to his cock, rubbing the head up and down against my pussy. I felt myself getting wet. This time I couldn't resist touching him. But as I went to do so, he grabbed my hands again, pulling them above my head once more, and kissed me again. I loved the way he dominated me, the forcefulness in his touch. There was no hesitation in his movements, no awkwardness. I gave myself completely to him. I turned towards the platform and leaned over it. Mark put his arms around me from behind. I felt his hard cock on my ass.

'Wait a second,' I said. I reached towards my kitbag. 'I have to get a condom.'

Suddenly he pulled away. He had been just seconds from thrusting his cock inside me. Now I feared that the fumbling for a condom had broken the flow.

'Don't need one. Let me just give you a massage,' he said. He sounded apologetic. 'Is that OK?'

I got the sense he was having second thoughts, so I turned towards him, sat on the platform, and took his cock in my mouth. He held the back of my head in one hand and pulled me into him. I felt him get rock hard right away. He seemed on the verge of coming, but I wanted to take my time so pulled away. His cock stood straight out, at a right angle to the rest of his body. It was pointed right at my face, as though demanding I take it back in my mouth.

'OK, I'll have that massage now,' I said, and, without waiting for a response, lay on my stomach.

Mark crawled on top of me, crouching on his knees and pinning my legs together between his own. He reached for a bottle of baby oil he had brought with him, and I heard him squeeze some liquid out and rub his hands together before applying the warm oil to my back. His hands moved in long strokes, sliding from the top of my shoulders down to my lower back. I wanted to feel his cock swing gently against my ass and his fingers part my legs. I lifted myself up slightly as he worked his way down my body, offering myself to him. But he resisted. Instead, he moved his hands up and down my body, up and down, before concentrating on my buttocks. Finally, he spread the cheeks open.

'You know, I'd love your cock in my ass,' I said, giving in to my desires. I waited for his fingers to brush against my clit.

'Do you mind if I just give you a massage?' he said.

'Just a massage?' I tried not to sound disappointed.

'Yes, just a massage,' he said. He sounded diffident. I got the sense he wanted to give me more than a massage.

'Can I turn over, then?' I said.

'If you want.'

I rolled over to face him. I was still between his legs, and now I could see his hard-on standing straight out. 'Can you just rub my pussy? Just a little?' I asked. 'I'm incredibly horny.'

'Yes, I can do that,' he said, as though concluding that that act was in the 'Allowed' column of his rule book. He began to finger me gently, first using his whole hand to rub the mound, then moving his fingers inside and out whilst applying pressure to my clit with his thumb.

It felt great, for about five minutes. 'Why won't you fuck me?' I said at last, feeling myself dripping on his hands, my pussy opening up more and more to receive his fingers. 'Is it the condoms?'

'No,' he said. 'It's just that … it would be cheating on my girlfriend. I can't do that.'

I let his comment go. I wasn't about to get involved in a conversation about the dynamics of his relationship. I just wanted to get off.

Mark's fingers continued dancing around my clit. The endorphins built, built until the desire to feel him inside me was so strong, I knew that his not fucking me wasn't an option. I raised myself up, put my arms around his lower back, and pulled his cock towards me, taking him in my mouth again. He kept his hand on my clit and continued rubbing. I pulled his cock completely into my mouth; I used my tongue to lap at the underside of his shaft, covering it with my saliva. I was lost in the pleasure of feeling his hands probing me and his cock inside my mouth.

Suddenly, Mark pulled me by the back of my hair, pushed me down onto the mat, and climbed on top of me, thrusting his tongue into my mouth. I felt his hard cock just inches away from my pussy. I grabbed his hips and pulled him inside. This time, he did not resist. He plunged into me, filling me up. I gasped.

I felt a rush of endorphins, almost like when I'm about to come, except I wasn't there yet. But it was a moment of such intense pleasure, so intoxicating that an orgasm was beside the point. Mark continued holding me down by my hair. It wasn't violent, it wasn't painful, but somehow it seemed right, given the force of his desire.

He pinned my right arm above my head, and with his free hand reached down for my left hand and locked his fingers around mine. His tongue never left my mouth. We were joined, every twitch of his cock, every thrust, seemed to connect to something inside me. Though we had been in a red room once before, this time was completely different.

He had only been fucking me for about five minutes, but I noticed that his balls had retracted, because they no longer slapped against me. He was getting closer.

'Please. Come inside me,' I said. I wanted him to fill me up, even though I knew it was stupid and reckless.

'Are you sure?'

'Yes. Please.' I arched my back to receive him, to take him in fully. He wasn't huge, but his obvious enjoyment was contagious. And I had wanted this since our last time together. I thought he was so sexy, and his touch so sensual, that for a change size didn't matter.

I felt the twitch that heralds a man's coming orgasm, then the rush of warm spunk inside me. His orgasm seemed to go on for minutes, seemingly as long as we'd been fucking. His body shuddered again and again, and his thrusts got deeper and faster. My pussy pulsated in time with his orgasm, contracting over and over. I was in no rush for him to stop.

When the pulsating finally stopped, we lay still for a while, my right arm still above my head and my left hand still entwined in his.

He kissed me gently, then rose up on his elbows and looked into my eyes.

Suddenly, I felt the need to reassure him that it was OK, that I was clean. 'I was tested recently,' I said. 'And I'm fine.'

'I'm clean too. I had my tests not long ago, and I haven't had sex in four months.'

'I don't usually do that,' I continued, feeling the need to confess. 'Never do that, in fact. That's why I tried to grab a condom from my bag.'

He climbed off me and moved to my side, propping himself up with one arm while stroking my body with his other hand.

'So, what's with the four-month thing?' I asked. 'How can you have a girlfriend and not have sex for four months?'

'She lives in Slovakia,' he said, rolling his eyes.

'Wow, that's one hell of a long-distance relationship,' I said. 'I tried that once. All I got out of it was some great phone sex and a lot of frustration.'

'Yeah, me too,' he said. 'But after a while phone sex gets boring.'

'And expensive.'

Mark smiled. 'Hey, I'm sorry. I don't usually come that quickly.'

'That's OK,' I said, and I meant it. There's a time for taking things slowly, and then there are times when passion and excitement set their own agenda. Sex with Mark was one such time; it was just what I'd wanted. I began to finger his nipple ring, something I'd not even noticed during our lovemaking.

'What does your girlfriend think of this thing?'

'I don't think I'll have a girlfriend for much longer,' he said. 'The long-distance thing doesn't work. It's just a ball-buster.'

For a minute I started to wonder whether there was any possibility for meeting Mark outside of Rio's. He wasn't a bad catch. But I quickly came back to reality. Relationships don't begin with a quickie in the red room. Mark didn't ask for my phone number and I didn't give him mine. That's just the way it is. As they say about Vegas, what happens there, stays there. But I hoped I'd see him again and knew that I would.

'OK, Suzanne' he said, giving me a quick kiss on the lips. 'See you around.'

As Mark walked out the door, I suddenly thought of James, who had asked me if a blowjob from a colleague constituted cheating on his wife. He wanted reassurance, I now realised, and I hadn't given it to him. Had I been playing according to Mark's rules, I would have said no. Giving me a back rub, kissing me, massaging my clit – none of that mattered to Mark. Even a blowjob in a couple's room didn't count. To most people, just walking through the door of a swinging club was crossing the line. It was only when his penis entered another woman that Mark felt he'd broken the rules. I'd not seen James for about six months and wondered if he had a second mobile number at this point, and more stories about car park blowjobs.

We all break our own rules. That Sunday with Mark, I'd even broken mine. I had allowed a man to fuck me without a condom. I came to the conclusion that, when it comes to sex, we're all full of shit.

5. YOUNGER MEN

I never understood the appeal of younger men until I met Kafele. Twenty-seven years old, five-foot ten and slim, he had the body of a footballer and a thick seven-inch cock, and he could make me come just by swivelling his hips for a few minutes. In or out of bed, he moved like a dancer, perhaps because music was his preferred form of communication. Which was just as well, since he knew only about 25 words of English, and of those, about half were related to sex or human anatomy, introduced into his vocabulary by me.

Originally from Senegal, he had recently come to the UK on a music sponsorship to teach the kora, a complicated African instrument that looked like an oddly shaped guitar and sounded like a harp. It is a beautiful instrument. And so was Kafele. I fell for him the moment I saw him.

Nadia had invited me to Momo for a catch-up, as we'd not seen each other for weeks. A Senegalese band was playing on the stage, and their music sounded lovely, but I didn't pay much attention at first. I was trying to flag down the cocktail waitress who was flirting with the bartender. My children had just gone off to upstate New York for a month at summer camp, and I wanted to celebrate my liberation. I'd been taking advantage of my new-found freedom by going out most nights and seeing friends.

After ordering a glass of rosé, I turned towards the stage and noticed a handsome black man sitting just a few feet away from my table, at the front of the stage. He was wearing traditional African clothing: a brightly patterned knee-length kaftan, loose black cotton under-trousers, and sandals. The big drum that formed the bottom part of his kora was wedged like a phallic totem between his legs.

I was wearing a black-and-white polka-dot dress and a pair of red high heels. It was an outfit better suited to a burlesque show than a Moroccan drinking club, but then Momo was meant to be a pit stop, a quick hello to Nadia before heading over to Modern Times, a retro cabaret at the Café Royal in Piccadilly.

As the kora player performed, I couldn't stop staring at him and, I couldn't help noticing, he at me. Smiling and swaying along to the music, I listened intently, watching his graceful hands move up and down the strings. His fingers moved so quickly, yet so sensuously, I wondered what they would feel like on my body. When Nadia came over during the break, I leaned across the table and said quietly, nodding towards the stage, 'He's gorgeous.'

'Who?' she said.

'That one,' I said, pointing to the kora player.

'Oh, yes, darling' she said. 'He's sweet.'

'I don't know about "sweet" but he's absolutely beautiful.'

When Nadia went back to her mixing desk and the musicians returned for their second set, my eyes went back to the stage.

As I watched my kora player, I worked up a chat-up line for after the show.

When the performance was over, the band left the stage. Just as I began wondering if I'd ever see the kora player again, he emerged from back-stage left wearing a pale-blue patterned shirt and dark trousers. Now he looked more like the footballers whose pictures my sons hung on their bedroom walls than an African musician.

I watched as the kora player walked over to the bar. Shortly afterwards, Nadia came up to my table. 'He wants to meet you,' she said.

'What did you say to him?' I asked, equal parts suspicious and delighted.

'Nothing, darling!' she said. Her tone sounded a bit too innocent.

'Yeah, right,' I replied, laughing. I knew Nadia well enough to figure she'd probably said a little more than nothing.

I walked up to the bar under the pretence of ordering another drink. 'A glass of rosé,' I said to the barman. Then I turned to the kora player. 'I really liked your playing.'

'Thank you, *merci*,' he said. He was softly spoken, with a pleasing French-African accent. He hung his head slightly, then shyly glanced up at me. 'You are beautiful.'

'Thank you.' My mother taught me that when a girl gets a compliment, her job is to say those two simple words, and then change the subject. It's rude to disagree, she said. I'm an attractive 46-year-old, a 34DD, size 12 (size 8 in the US, as I liked to remind myself, that lower number sounding so much better). I've got good legs and a firm ass, thanks to a decade with a tough personal trainer. Unlike a lot of other women my age, I never wear make-up – or underwear, for that matter. I've never had Botox, nor even pondered any kind of surgical reconstruction. I'm counting on my good genes to see me through – even in their seventies, my parents look ten years younger than their age – if only because a lifelong fear of needles means I will probably never go under the knife. I'm no supermodel, but I'm quite all right.

I hadn't heard that chat-up line in a long time. If only all men knew those three words was all they needed to say to a girl. 'What's your name?' I asked.

'Kafele,' he said.

'Nice to meet you, Kafilly.'

'Kafele.' He smiled.

'OK,' I replied. 'Kah-*feh*-leh.' His was the kind of name I tended to forget instantly. Not Hugh, not Nigel. 'Kafele. Kafele.' I have a terrible memory for names, and foreign ones have an especially poor chance of sinking in. Thus my frequent employment of the all-purpose 'sweetheart'.

Cuban music was screaming out of the speakers, its salsa beat so appealing. 'Would you like to dance?' I said.

'Yes.' Kafele took my hand and led me to the middle of the restaurant, which now served as a dance floor. His feet instantly moved to the three-step rhythm. He held me close. Soon we were not just touching, but rubbing up against each other. Kafele was very slim, but I saw that his forearms were nicely toned and felt firm biceps under his short-sleeved shirt. Drummer's arms. Then, as he pushed his body into mine, I felt his six-pack and pecs. And I felt his cock get hard.

When the song ended, I leaned in to kiss Kafele. He did not pull away. His tongue moved to find mine, and his soft lips pressed against my own. I put my hand around the back of his neck and pulled him into me. I felt his hard-on again. As his tongue grew more insistent, I became aware of myself getting wet. We kissed for four or five minutes, which is to say, about a week in public-space time. We remained in the middle of the dance floor.

'Do you live near?' he asked at last.

'I have a car,' I said. 'Would you like to come back with me?'

'I like that.'

We left the club and walked to my car. It was parked in Golden Square, about five minutes away. The two of us walked hand in hand, like schoolchildren.

'This is nice car,' he said when I pressed the key fob to release the locks on the doors.

'Thanks,' I said. 'It's a BMW 118. But it's not mine, it's a lease.'

'OK. Very nice.'

I wasn't sure if he understood what I had said, but suddenly remembering that his English was limited, I pulled a Trojan music compilation out of the glove compartment and put it in the player so we didn't have to talk much.

Twenty minutes later, we were inside my house. Five minutes after that, we were naked in bed.

I hadn't asked how old Kafele was, and I didn't want to know. Looking at his smooth brown skin, his hard, hairless body and his fine features, I guessed he could have been anywhere between nineteen and thirty and, even if thirty, that would have made him nearly young enough to be my son. That is not exactly a turn-on for me. From my limited experience of sleeping with younger men, I've learned three things:

1. Young men have their limits as lovers. They can get it up faster and keep it up longer than older men, but they lack the sexual finesse of a more-experienced man.

2. Their cultural references are at odds with mine. The proof added up over the years, of course, as, one by one, boys I met didn't know who Bobby Sherman was, couldn't sing along to 'One Less Bell to Answer', didn't understand the reference to the 'Robert Palmer-video chick' look. I gave up on boy-toys after telling a guy two decades my junior that I'd always regretted not going to the Roxy to see Johnny Rotten with my classmates. 'Wasn't he the guy –' I should have known this was coming '– in *I'm a Celebrity Get Me Out of Here!?*'

3. They are expensive. While they're still climbing the career ladder, I'm close to the top. That means I've learned to eat at decent restaurants, and am expected to pay if I want to bring along someone young enough to wear bell-bottoms without irony.

Kafele was different, at least in some important ways. He made up for his lack of language skills with bedroom skills, as I learned during our first night together. As a lover, he was hardly an amateur. When we fucked, he moved and led as if we were still dancing. Our hips rotated in time to our own tempo, even our tongues, touching and darting and circling, worked like well-rehearsed partners. Kafele said little when we fucked. He didn't really need to. The sex was so fluid, words were unnecessary.

'You don't talk very much, do you?' I said the second time we screwed in silence.

'I talk with the body,' he said.

And he did. He was not a graduate of the Hard and Fast School of Sex. He seemed never to be in a rush. I loved it when he sucked and licked my nipples and caressed my skin. He was sensuous, not rough, and, like most men of his generation, he could keep it up for hours. He was sweet, devoted to my pleasure. Perhaps that's why his most memorable act in the bedroom was holding my ass open while watching himself take me from behind. He would rise up, push away from me with his arms, and position himself for a better view. That was as kinky as he got, and even that wasn't particularly kinky – not on my tricks continuum, anyway – but at least it was a diversion from the constant sweetness and attentiveness. His body was gorgeous and fucking him felt great, but there's only so many times I can do the missionary position with someone before I grow bored. Dark on the outside, vanilla between the sheets.

Still, he was a welcome stand-in for Karume, my ex-boyfriend. Karume, another sexy African, had called himself a one-woman man but his lies, I eventually learned, were as long as his dick. He lied regularly ('I'll be home by seven'), cheated on me ('That's not lipstick'), stole my car ('I just moved it closer to the house'), couldn't hold a job ('My boss is an asshole'), and then lied some more. He was trouble. But I stuck with him for a year, on and off, and even let him move in for three months, because he was kind of kinky, so the sex was always fresh. After Karume, I wanted a break from brain damage and welcomed being with a person who was happy to just be with me, without having to say a word.

One night I sat on Kafele's chest and stared down at him, taking in his youthful face and body. I stroked his broad shoulders, his rippled chest, his narrow waist. His hard body, along with the contrast of his brown skin against my own pale flesh, was arousing. I pinched his nipples playfully. He stared up at me with his big brown eyes.

'You are very beautiful,' I said.

'*Merci*. Thank you,' he said. Then he laughed and thrust his pelvis playfully into me.

I moaned. 'That feels too good,' I said. 'If you don't stop it, Kafele, you're going to make me come. I don't want to come just yet.' It was only fifteen minutes after we'd climbed into bed. 'Can you eat my pussy?' I said.

He squinted his eyes and looked at me. The furrow of his brow made clear his lack of understanding.

'Eat ... my ... pussy,' I repeated.

'Pardon?'

'Eat.' I stood up on my knees and began inching up his chest. 'My.' I moved closer. Then I thrust my pelvis to make my point. 'Pussy.'

'I am sorry,' he said. 'I do not understand.'

I'd never had to play sexual charades before and felt a little self-conscious sticking out my tongue. 'Eat,' I said, pointing to my tongue, moving it left and right. Then I pointed at my pussy. 'My . . .'

'Ah!' he said.

'Yes!' I said.

'Oh,' he said. 'OK.' I climbed off him and lay on my back. Kafele crawled between my legs and began gently rolling his tongue around. 'Like this?'

'Yes,' I said. I was relieved that I didn't have to explain the *how* of it.

I felt myself getting wet within seconds, and then the urge to be filled took over. I climbed back on top of him.

He pushed into me again and within a minute my pussy started to pulsate around his cock. I came. Then Kafele turned me over and moved on top of me one more time. The aftershocks of my orgasm were still lingering as I felt his cock harden, felt his breath quicken.

'*Oui*! *Oui*!,' he said. '*Ouais*!' His come poured into me.

Kafele lay on top of me a few minutes longer and buried his face in my neck. Then he rolled over and wrapped an arm around me. We kissed. It was a sweet and gentle moment, as all moments with Kafele were.

'You are lovely,' he said. '*Tu est belle.*'

'So are you,' I said. 'Lovely . . .' My last words before falling asleep.

Although Kafele had lived in the UK less than a year, he came off like someone who'd stepped off the plane just a day before. It was refreshing being with someone who had never heard of Donny Williams, didn't read lad's mags or follow *Big Brother* or even know what *Desperate Housewives* was. It didn't matter that he didn't understand the cultural references from my youth. Even a few hours with him was like a holiday, worlds removed from my celebrity-drenched working life with an entertainment company. He didn't smoke, didn't drink, didn't take drugs. He only drank water when we went out. But he didn't seem to mind my ordering one, then another, mojito or glass of rosé, and maybe another after that.

We carried on seeing each other for three months. We hooked up three times a week, initially, which for me felt almost like being married, as it had been years since I'd fucked anyone other than Karume so regularly. But after six weeks, I got bored and started making excuses, till we were getting together only once every other week. In part this was because a kinky new playmate, Carl, unexpectedly came into my life.

I met Carl at the Night of the Senses, a party for perverts that follows the Erotic Awards, awards given to artists, photographers, sex workers, websites, basically anything connected to sex and the sex industry in the UK. I almost didn't go to the event, but I had spontaneously told my friend Tania, who was volunteering, as I had for five years running, to sign me up as well. As the big night drew nearer, I was regretting the offer of my time – and my big mouth. Tania and I had made plans to hit the after-party together, and I debated just staying home for some easy sex with Kafele.

But I'd committed. So I drove to the Renaissance Rooms in Vauxhall, where the event was being held that year, and performed my duties, in the name of solidarity with like-minded sex-positive folk. Then I went into the after-party space to find Tania. I spied Claire, a fellow volunteer I'd worked with over the years, standing against the wall. She was wearing a vintage 1950s one-piece swimsuit and some 1940s platform shoes. Her shoulder-length black hair was pulled back into pigtails. Petite and cute, just over five-feet tall, she was a little pixie who could pass for 25 any day of the week, even though she was at least a decade older. But in the dim light, she almost looked like jailbait.

'So, seen any action yet?' I asked. The party was always an anything-goes affair, complete with play areas with names like Fetish Palace, Massage Garden, Anything Goes Den, Women's Swoon Space, Boys' Back Room, Roissy Dungeon, in fact pretty much anything designed for adult pleasures. Yet, strangely, I didn't feel much electricity in the air. Every year I'd gone, I'd seen the same bald man get fisted by the same overweight woman spilling out of the same PVC leotard; seen the same droopy-tit woman in cheap chain-mail pissing on the same scrawny senior citizen in, probably, the same children's paddling pool. Though a full range of perversion and perversity was available to me, and I could have found something, somewhere, that might appeal, as a sex venue Night of the Senses didn't really work for me. I was always more successful at sex parties and small swingers' clubs. Typically, there's less female competition in those places, since women are hesitant to go to saunas, sex clubs and swinging parties on their own, and that means more men for me.

'Action?' said Claire. 'Not really interested in any of this. But I'm going backstage in five minutes to help Rump Shaker prepare for his act.'

'Prepare?' I said, raising an eyebrow. 'Rump Shaker?'

'He's one of the strippers,' she said. 'He needs to get hard before he goes on stage. And I'm going to help him.'

'Hmm,' I said, approvingly.

'The thing is,' she continued, all wide-eyed and innocent 'it's so big that I really could use some help.'

'How big?' I said.

She held her hands about ten inches apart.

'Do you think *I* could help you? I am a volunteer here, after all.'

'That would be great!' she said. 'Meet me backstage in five.'

Slowly I made my way to the backstage area, thrilled that I might actually get something that year. I stopped en route to watch the PVC-clad dom fist her partner, to kill a few minutes.

'I don't get it,' I said, mainly to myself.

'That's nothing,' said the scrawny little guy in a leather thong standing next to me. 'You just missed the real show. A few minutes ago, there were three women with their hand up his ass, all at the same time.'

'I just don't get it,' I said again.

'Nor do I,' he said. 'But he looked like he was enjoying it.'

'Oh, that's the guy who likes getting fisted,' said a familiar voice next to me.

I turned to see Tania. She looked great. About five-foot eight, curvy, with shoulder-length chestnut hair and fantastic tits, she was wearing a red tight-fitting top with straps that criss-crossed her chest, accentuating her boobs, and a short leather miniskirt and ankle boots.

'Seems so,' I said. 'Hi! *You* seen any action here yet?'

'No,' she said. 'The last time I saw any action here was a couple of years ago. I snogged this guy. He was actually really nice. I should have gotten his number.' She sounded wistful, romantic, as if speaking about a bloke she met on a picnic in Hyde Park, and not some perv from a full-on sex party. 'You?'

'I'm on my way backstage to help Rump Shaker prepare for his act. Apparently it's really big – his cock, I mean I don't know about the act. Wanna come and watch?'

'Sure,' she said. 'Sounds fun.'

On the way to the backstage area, we passed the swingers' tent and a flautist playing classical music and a pole-dancing stripper and the geriatric being pissed on and climbed over cables and detoured around a makeshift clothes rail dripping with glittery strippers' costumes. Finally we reached what was clearly the dressing room, a small space with one wall handily lined with mirrors. The long counter against it was covered with make-up, hairdryers, curling tongs, overflowing ashtrays and empty beer bottles, evidence of all the strippers and artistes who had been there earlier. It was otherwise empty, including no Claire, aside from a naked black man sitting in an old wooden chair with his back to us. I could tell from his hand movement he was wanking.

Tania and I exchanged a smile.

I cleared my throat and walked towards him. He didn't react to my footsteps, perhaps thinking they belonged to one of the dozens of pros working and sharing the room that night. I felt slightly nervous. Despite having blown scores of guys in swingers' clubs and at my neighbourhood sauna – students, builders, bakers, journalists, musicians, taxi drivers, cops, lawyers, IT wonks – I'd never met a stripper before, much less blown one. In my mind he was a professional and presumably met gorgeous strippers all the time through his work. I assumed he only went out with perfect bodies and perfect tits. I may have felt hot that night – push-up tits and six-inch hooker shoes – but as I reminded myself while moving towards the chair, I was, as they say, no spring chicken.

Rump Shaker looked up.

I was now standing in front of him, facing him, or rather, facing it. It was hard to miss. Thick, hard and, yes, about ten inches: a very attractive cock. He continued what he was doing, which, I could now see, was wrapping leather cord around the base of the shaft, which I assumed helped him stay hard, and made the show more titillating for the audience.

He was bald, with high cheekbones and big brown eyes, very good looking. His shoulders were broad and he had completely smooth, hairless skin, plus great abs and thick, muscular thighs. He was perfectly proportioned in every way. The diamond stud in his front tooth was a ghetto-trash touch, kind of tacky, as was the silver lightning bolt glued onto an incisor. But, hey, I thought, this is just a blowjob, I'm not going out with this guy, I'm not going to marry him, I don't need to introduce him to my parents. This is just plain fun. And a first, for me – action at the Erotic Awards.

I looked at his cock and then into his eyes. 'Claire tells me you could use some help,' I said provocatively.

Rump Shaker stared into my face for a few seconds, then moved his eyes down my body. He paused over my breasts, which were popping out of a clingy Lycra leopard-print halter-neck dress, then dropped down to my waist, slim and toned, then to my legs, wrapped in slutty fishnet stockings, and settled on my six-inch red patent wedge-heeled shoes. 'Yes,' he said, looking up. 'I *could* use some help.'

'Would you like *me* to help you,' I said.

'Yes,' he said, smiling, 'I would.'

I crouched down until my mouth was level with his cock. I leaned in and ran my tongue from the base to the head before sliding him into my mouth. Claire was right. He was big. Not too big for my taste, but too big to fit completely in my mouth, so I slid my hand down the shaft of his cock whilst letting my tongue work the top. He stood up and reached behind my head, pulling me into him.

'Mmm,' he said. 'That's really good.'

I pulled out his cock and said seductively, looking up at him, 'I'm only here to help.' I used my hand to jerk him off.

'I did need help,' he said with a laugh.

'I know,' I said, smiling. 'Too bad Claire didn't come. Her loss.'

I took him back in my mouth, closing my eyes, relaxing into the rhythm, and let him into my mouth deeper and deeper. Shania Twain's 'I Feel Like a Woman' played in the background.

I heard other people enter the room. They stood at the entrance, by Tania, who was watching my technique from afar.

'Lucky bloke!' shouted one guy.

'Tell me about it, man,' I heard Rump Shaker say. 'She gives a fucking brilliant blowjob.'

I ignored the comments.

'Hey, babe, that's great,' he said softly, pulling out suddenly. He stroked my hair. 'I better get dressed. I have to go on in a minute.'

'No problem.' I kissed him on the lips. 'Always happy to help.'

I stood up and adjusted my dress. It had slid up my thighs while I'd been crouching down. I walked over to Tania and together we walked out the door and around the corner of the hall, then stood by the side of the stage to watch Rump Shaker perform.

A few minutes later, Nelly's 'Hot In Herre' started playing, loudly. The curtain rustled and Rump Shaker stepped out. He was dressed in a British policeman's uniform, with shiny, tight black trousers, a tight white shirt, a long black tie and a bobby's cap on top. He smiled broadly as he strutted around the stage, swinging a truncheon to the beat. He looked so confident, so comfortable onstage, lapping up the attention from the women and men in the audience. Many were hooting and cheering, and all were waiting for the fantasy cop to reveal his manhood. I felt secretly empowered, as if the performer and I shared a secret.

The audience wasn't kept in suspense for very long. Two minutes into the song starting, Rump Shaker had ripped off his uniform and was down to a chain-mail thong. Soon after that, he was naked, and his hard cock was protruding out from his body like a missile. He reached into the audience and pulled a woman onto the stage. The crowd hollered. Rump Shaker put his hands on his partner's shoulders and pushed her down on all fours, like a dog, then crouched behind her, rubbing himself against her, simulating sex.

Just a few minutes ago, he was in my mouth, I thought. *I'm* the one who got him hard.

As if reading my thoughts, Tania looked at me and said, 'Good blowjob, Suzanne.'

I felt naughty whilst watching the man I'd fluffed, a fantasy bobby to everyone else there, strut around the stage.

He grabbed another woman from the audience and, putting a collar around her neck, fastened it to a leash he held in one hand. I recognised the woman as a stripper I'd seen perform earlier in the evening. She played along, crawling across the stage wherever Rump Shaker led her, his huge cock pointing the way. Watching his act was making me horny. The pre-show fluffing had been exciting. Now I wanted more.

When the performance ended, Rump Shaker took a bow. Then he collected his clothes, now scattered around the stage, threw everything into a black duffel bag, and walked backstage. I followed.

'Nice show,' I said, as I entered the dressing room. 'Would you like me to finish you off?'

He was hot and sweaty. Perspiration was dripping off his body and he was breathing hard.

'Of course.' He spoke as casually as if he'd just been offered a glass of water. He leaned against the make-up counter.

Ignoring the others in the room, I grabbed a condom from my bag and swiftly rolled it on. My mouth followed, to get him harder. Then I lifted my skirt, revealing my shaved pussy, bent over the messy countertop, and thrust my ass in the air. I put my head down and closed my eyes. Your turn to service me, I thought.

I felt the tip of his cock start to enter me, stretching my vagina. A few seconds later, I felt someone else's fingers reach underneath me to stroke my clit. I didn't look up or say a word.

'Nice ass,' said a man whose voice I didn't recognise.

'Yeah, man,' agreed Rump Shaker whilst pumping me. 'She's a beauty.'

Soon I heard more people enter the room. I looked up and saw we had a little audience.

A couple of guys and a couple of girls approached.

'That's horny,' said one of the men.

'Definitely the horniest thing going on here,' agreed one of the girls, laughing. Apparently, like me, she'd been unimpressed by what was on offer elsewhere.

We carried on fucking, oblivious to our fans.

'Suck me off,' said Rump Shaker, pulling out of me after a few more minutes.

I turned around and crouched down, like I'd done before his number. I unrolled the condom from his cock and threw it on the floor. Once again, I took him in my mouth, jerking him off with alternating hands. He was too big for me to continuously suck. I found myself gagging when he tried pushing his cock farther into my mouth. Again, I was reminded of Claire. She was right; he really was too much for one woman.

Five minutes on, I felt his cock stiffen and the warm spunk shoot down my throat.

'Thanks,' he said as he pulled out. 'That was fucking great.'

'You're welcome,' I said, laughing. Once again I rose off my knees, adjusted my skirt, and walked out the door.

I found Tania by the side of the stage, where I'd left her. She was watching a female stripper's pole dance.

'You looked like you were having fun,' she said. 'I popped backstage a bit ago and caught the end of your show. Good technique.'

'Thanks,' I said, taking the compliment. 'I think I'm gonna go. It's not going to get better than that for me.'

'I think you're right,' she said. 'I'm going to stick around for a while. I'll ring you tomorrow and let you know if I got lucky.'

I found my coat, which I'd stuffed under one of the tables. Relieved that no one had stolen it or used it as a mattress, I put it on and walked out to my car, thinking of Rump Shaker.

I wanted to see him again. It was rare to meet someone with such a perfectly formed body. Rare, too, to find someone whose cock felt so great inside me. Although we'd exchanged only a few words, I liked his laid-back attitude. I also liked the way he'd looked me up and down. Now, all I had to do was find out his real name and get his number.

I drove home and went to bed. As I drifted off to sleep, sweet, young Kafele came to mind. He was coming round mid-morning for a 'wake up'.

6. SWEET, NOT SPICY

While I waited for Kafele to come round for a morning quickie, I put in a call to my best mate, Pat, to fill her in on the night before.

'I can't believe you, Suzanne,' she said, as I described, between mouthfuls of Rice Krispies, meeting and then shagging a stripper with a big fat cock. 'I hope you got his number.'

I told her I hadn't done. 'Don't even know his real name,' I said. 'All I know is that they call him Rump Shaker.'

'I doubt you'll find that listed in the phone book.'

I didn't think getting his real name would be difficult. There were plenty of people I knew from the Erotic Awards after volunteering for so many years, and I figured someone would come through. And if not, I could call a strip-a-gram agency and put in a request.

'I'll find him,' I said. 'How many six-foot-tall, totally ripped, ten-inch-cocked black strippers with a diamond in their front tooth are there? It's a niche!'

'I don't know how you do it, Suzanne. I wouldn't have the guts to proposition someone I didn't know,' said Pat. 'Or afterwards be able to say goodbye, come to think of it. I mean, a guy with a body like that, how do you disconnect?'

'It just felt right,' I explained, 'closing off the fantasy by walking out when it was over. Except I wouldn't mind connecting again, I must say.'

'That's what I mean, Suzanne.'

'Well, I don't know anything about him. He could have a girlfriend, be married. But I'll give it a shot, Pat, and let you know.' I laughed.

'What about Kafele? I thought you really liked him.' Pat's question was a jolt, reminding me my kora player would be ringing my door for a rendezvous at any minute.

'C'mon, Pat,' I said. 'That is never going to be serious. The guy's just a kid. He's only twenty-seven. I'm just a pit stop until he finds a girl closer to his own age.'

'Have you two talked about this?'

'Not really. It is what it is,' I said. 'Anyway, we don't really talk much. He doesn't know much English, remember?'

Kafele and I had settled into a pattern. We'd get together every few weeks for dinner and sex at my house, and afterwards usually watch an action movie from my sons' collection of plot-lite, big-bang Hollywood extravaganzas. It worked out all right, at first. As a musician, he didn't have much money, so my dinners helped him out. He liked American movies, so the few words he heard over the guns and car crashes probably helped his English. And I got at least one orgasm out of each rendezvous, which helped take the edge off.

After a while it became almost tedious, though. Kafele wasn't adventurous in the sack. The sex became monotonous. So I tried to spice up our trysts.

'Would you slip your cock up my ass?' I asked one night.

'*Excuse-moi*?' he asked.

Here we go again, I thought. Another game of charades. I pointed to his cock. Then I pointed to my bum.

'Oh,' he said, pulling away from me. 'No. No.'

I knew nothing was going to change. Yet, just as I'd find myself ready to call it off, I'd think about how Kafele would grow hard as soon as he walked through the door and stay hard through the night – even during the obligatory movie, when I fondled him – and then I'd end up giving him a ring.

Meeting Rump Shaker at the Erotic Awards after a couple of months with Kafele confirmed for me that, sweet as he was, my kora player would never play a big part in my life. He was like a wholesome vacation in the country, a temporary break from the real world – my world, anyway, which was oral and anal, full of toys and boys, and swinging clubs and saunas and orgies and one-night stands. Kafele would never go for that, or even understand it; besides, I didn't even want to introduce him to the scene. Up until the Awards, I'd kept that other side of my life worlds away from him and tried playing the perfect girlfriend. But it was just an act.

'I knew a guy like that,' said my friend Aidan as I described our relationship. Aidan was a music promoter, and I figured it was likely he'd come across a few African musicians whilst touring with bands over the years, so I called him up and invited him to lunch at the Electric, a members-only restaurant on Portobello Road which is popular with arts-and-media types.

'I would never take him to the clubs or things like the Erotic Awards,' he said. 'They're too outside his own experience.' Aidan told me about being on tour in the 80s with a famous band that had recruited an African drummer as part of their show. He said the drummer had never had an alcoholic drink before the tour started, but by the end of it, he was wandering the streets, crying and miserable, having got hooked on vodka and cocaine. Aidan had to fly him back home to his family.

'Just have a nice time together,' he counselled. 'Stay at home. Cook for him. Watch the telly. Take it from me. Anything else is not a good idea.'

It depressed me a little that, even before hearing Aidan's advice, I'd been following it. I'd kept quiet about the Erotic Awards, gone on my own, and that's how I'd ended up blowing Rump Shaker. And wanting to see the stripper again.

Till that happened, there was wholesome, vanilla Kafele. I sent him a text message. 'How's your day going?'

My phone vibrated when he replied. 'I not eating.'

God, I thought, things must really be bad if he can't afford food.

I debated inviting him round for a meal, but it was a weeknight, my kids were home, and they had never met Kafele. After Karume left our lives, I'd stuck to my pledge not to introduce boyfriends to my boys. I didn't want them growing attached again to someone who might not stick around for long.

'Why aren't you eating?' I texted back.

'I am Muslim,' he replied.

It was a relief knowing he wasn't skint.

'I'm a non-practising Jew,' I shot back. 'Maybe together we can sort out world peace.'

I hadn't figured Kafele for the religious type at all. I'd never seen him pray. He'd never mentioned any Islamic religious festivals. He didn't smoke or drink, but that hadn't struck me as particularly unusual. His staying sober all the time had seemed to reflect an impressive dedication to his music. He was non-stop horny and spent most of his time in bed whenever he was with me. He worshipped my body, so porking a Jewish woman old enough to be his mother didn't exactly seem . . . observant.

Never having dated a Muslim guy, I went on Google for some Ramadan 101, which led to Koran 101.

I worked out that, as a divorcee, I was considered impure. That didn't bother me, as I assumed it meant he could do pretty much whatever he wanted with my filthy body, short of fucking me up the ass. I was fine to screw, but not to marry. So I figured I was a pretty safe bet for a young horny Muslim guy.

Except for the Ramadan bit. It turned out that the start of Ramadam meant that, firstly, he was not allowed to eat from sunrise to sunset, and, secondly, 'lascivious thoughts' were forbidden. That might prove problematic, so I rang him up.

'Is it true that for the next thirty days you're not allowed to have naughty thoughts?'

'Naughty thoughts?' he asked. I loved hearing his charming French-African accent.

'You know,' I said, wondering how to put it in simple English, 'thinking about sex. That sort of stuff.'

'Oh, it is OK,' he said. 'Just not in the day.'

Did that mean he could fuck me from sunset to sunrise, just not in the morning?

'Yes. That is right.'

'Oh, that's cool then.' Sort of. I was thinking how much I really liked morning sex.

'Sometimes, I have those thinkings after the breakfast.'

I smiled at Kafele's cheeky confession. But there was something about our conversation that got to me. As I hung up, I realised I wanted action, not *thinkings*. The scrambled syntax was cute, but it reminded me of what I'd been missing over the past three months. And it wasn't just sexual spontaneity. It was the ability to really communicate. Being with someone who was simple and honest and sweet was just what I'd needed after Karume. But suddenly I realised that I had moved on, from both of them. I needed a man who could tell me a joke, a guy who didn't need me to play charades in bed. I needed kinky.

I thought about Rump Shaker. In his business, being naughty came naturally. He was uninhibited, obviously, and fit and beautiful besides. Maybe not boyfriend material, but I wanted to taste something other than vanilla for a change. I wanted chocolate.

I called up my girlfriend Hannah. She's a stunning Australian who looks like a 1940s French movie star and reminded some of my friends of Kate Moss. She used to book acts at Torture Garden and had a Rolodex full of strippers and pole dancers.

Trying to sound innocent, I asked if she knew a stripper called Rump Shaker.

Knowing me like she did, she saw through my act in about two seconds. 'Oh, you mean Carl?' she said. 'Horny are we, Suzanne?'

'I don't know his name,' I said. 'He was called Rump Shaker at the Erotic Awards. He's got a diamond in his tooth.'

'Yeah, that's Carl.'

'You don't happen to have his number, do you? I sucked him off at the Awards and I would kinda like to do it again.'

She laughed. 'Nice guy, big cock. Been fucking around for years,' she said. 'Hold on, I'll get it for you.'

'Perfect!' I said. 'I've been playing goody-two-shoes for months and really need, you know, to let rip.'

'Good luck, babe,' she said. 'By the way, he usually likes to drag along his friend Paulie, too. Wild. Just don't say I didn't warn ya.'

7. STAR FUCKS

'He's hot!' Kate said. 'I mean, reeeeeally hot. Hot-hot-hot!' We were standing in the kitchen in my office, talking about the lead singer of a band she and some co-workers went to see at Shepherds Bush Empire the night before. I hadn't gone to the show, because when it comes to rock concerts, my policy is to stay away if not going VIP and guaranteed an upholstered chair. It was OK in my twenties, hanging out in clubs that reeked of last week's alcohol and a million cigarettes, standing up all night, drinking warm beer. But I am in my forties now, and it is all about comfort. I'd rather get spanked for two hours than have to stand up for one, crooking my neck for the occasional glimpse of a few skinny guys on a stage a mile away. At least in the spank-me position I'd have a comfortable lap to lie over.

'What's so hot about him?' I asked. I'd seen the guy's picture all over town, in advance of the band's European tour. He looked standard rock 'n' roll attractive to me: obligatory three-day-old stubble, short-cropped dyed-black hair, a half-dozen hideous tattoos. His face was cute, but almost too round – annoyingly youthful, it hadn't begun to sag even a bit. No muscle tone, no body fat, mostly just bones dressed in a pair of ripped jeans and a T-shirt. Yawn.

'He just is,' Kate said. 'He has real sex appeal. Even *I* fancy him.'

That was saying something. Kate is about 23, all tits, no ass, slim, with long light-brown hair and a classically pretty face. She took her hippie-chic dress cues from Sienna Miller, was well spoken and nice, and had been with the same guy for years, happily. So the thought of her even desiring another guy was revealing.

'Oh, you sound like one of those girls who looks at every guy in *Heat* magazine and says, "Ooh, he's cute, he's cute,"' I teased.

She laughed.

'Anyway, whatever. I don't see it,' I said. 'But I'll let you know what I think.' I looked at her meaningfully. 'I'll be spending all afternoon with him.'

The rock star's photo shoot with *Hello* magazine was arranged for 2.30. I'd booked the venue – the recently fabulousified Mayfair Hotel. I planned to arrive early, have a quick meet-and-greet with the photographer and his lighting guy, check out the locations to make sure they were suitable, and then await the rock star. As a type, they are problematic. They tend to arrive late, if at all, require lots of hand holding, alcohol and cigarettes, plus a shadow – someone to trail them, to make sure they don't trash the room.

But first I planned on a little R & R at Rio's, with my newly acquired, and now favourite, fuck buddy, Carl, a.k.a. Rump Shaker. Hannah had come through with the number, and it hadn't taken Carl long to come in me.

'Got a couple hrs to kill before appt later this afternoon,' I texted him. 'Any chance of a quickie?'

'Rio's. 12,' he texted back.

I told my staff I was off to the Mayfair.

Carl was waiting in reception as I walked in through the door. We had a quick shower and a steam, then walked upstairs to a private room. I closed the door so I could have Carl and his ten inches all to myself. I'd briefly contemplated a threesome after seeing a familiar face in one of the Jacuzzis. Michael was a guy I fucked from time to time. He was a Friday regular and had one of the fattest cocks I had ever seen. But that wasn't the only thing that put him on my radar. He loved licking pussy and, knowing Carl did not, I figured having the two of them in the same room might make for a perfect sandwich. Carl wouldn't have minded. Like Michael, he was a seasoned player.

But I changed my mind. I had to watch the clock, and had only about 45 minutes, hardly enough time to satisfy my need for some solo-time with Carl. I hadn't seen him for a couple of weeks and wanted to taste and suck on his beautiful cock. Michael's cock was world class, but Carl had the most handsome penis I'd ever seen. Michael's was a Coke can, but Carl's was like a sculpture, a piece of art. Just thinking about him, and it, brought me close to orgasm. 'Before I leave, I want to spunk in your mouth,' he said once, and those words stuck in my mind. Replaying them again and again, like an old 45, put me in a spin. It was as much the way he said it as the words themselves. He was comfortable with his own sexuality. He made wanting to come in my mouth sound as natural as ordering a pint of lager. I liked his lack of pretence and admired his confidence in his manhood. He was cool.

Carl lay down on the mat, and I took his soft cock in my mouth. I felt it get hard within minutes. It had a velvety smoothness, as pleasant, in its way, as the fuzzy texture of the nodding dog I had on my car dashboard.

He lay on his back with one hand behind his head and, even

though I had my eyes closed while I worked his cock, I knew he was watching me. I was crouching over him. He reached down to massage my clit gently, just the way he knew I liked it.

'Can I sit on top of you?' I asked. I'd been itching to grind on his cock since texting him that morning, since realising, for the first time, that grinding was about the one thing we hadn't done that was still on my to-do list. We'd done anal, sixty-nine, threesomes; we'd fucked in my hot tub and in my car and in front of a crowd, he'd spanked and flogged me; I'd nibbled on his balls. It wasn't the most extensive list, but then we'd only seen each other three or four times since meeting at the Erotic Awards.

I could tell from the way he smirked that the answer was yes.

I reached over to my kitbag, pulled out a condom, ripped it open with my teeth and put it over the tip of his cock. As ever, it strained to fit going down, he was that thick. I tried to gently slide the condom farther down, towards his balls. Seeing me struggle, Carl reached down and did it himself.

I mounted his cock and bore down on him, straining to take him inside despite being dripping wet. We rested, I bore down some more, we rested again, then I felt my pussy relax and he was in. Grinding down on him, I felt a surge of pleasure as my clit rubbed against his pelvic bone. Carl reached behind me and gently inserted a finger in my ass.

We kissed. His mouth was big, his lips soft. If you were gay, I thought, you'd be a hit on the circuit; hell, with that mouth, you could handle a cock as big as your own. He wasn't, though; guys weren't his thing. But he was the perfect stripper, willing to perform for anyone, male or female, and the perfect fuck buddy, ever ready to perform for me.

Carl's tongue circled my teeth and I felt his body arch in rhythm with mine. God, he felt so good. I grabbed his nipples and gently squeezed, feeling him get harder. Ten minutes later, I climaxed, screaming as I came.

I laughed. 'That's what I sound like when I have a really big orgasm,' I said. 'Now you know.'

I was feeling light-headed. I moved off Carl's body and removed the condom from his cock, then took him in my mouth again.

'Wow, that's … lovely,' he said as I took him as far into my mouth as I could. There were still another three inches to go, but I could not reach the base of his cock. I continued deep-throating him and then, as his balls retracted and his breath quickened, I began jerking him off. His come dripped over my hand and down the side of his cock. I lapped it up.

At 2.45, fashionably but not rudely late, the rock star walked through the hotel door with an entourage of two: his agent, a big name in the music industry, and his manager, a brassy, seen-it-all American broad about my age. My hair was still damp from a quick post-play shower at Rio's. I hoped nobody would pick up on the after-sex glow I was convinced exuded from every pore; I felt fluorescent.

I got off my chair and walked across the lobby to shake VZ's hand. 'Hi, I'm Suzanne,' I said.

'Hey, gorgeous,' said VZ, draping his arm around me. His greeting was so clichéd, it was like something out of a pick-up-artist handbook.

Kate had warned me about his flirtatiousness. She'd gone backstage after the previous night's show and had seen him in action. 'He is an outrageous flirt,' she said. 'He was coming on to all the girls – *all* the girls.' She thought it was funny.

I chose to ignore his greeting and got on with business. 'Right,' I said, turning away and gesturing towards the Amba Bar. 'The photographer's set up, waiting for you. It's gorgeous,' I said, looking at VZ. 'We've got a fantastic suite upstairs, too, for the other pictures. Follow me.'

VZ was exceptionally friendly during the introductions, making sure he got the photographer's, the photographer's assistant's, and the make-up artist's names, asking where they were from. A bit of an actor, a bit of a cad, but at least he had some manners.

After the hellos I proposed relocating to the suite, to meet the stylist and work out the clothes for each shot.

'Sounds good,' said the rocker. 'Lead the way, gorgeous.'

Gorgeous *this*, I thought. I walked towards the lifts, putting three feet between us so he could admire the back view.

The agent and manager were on their mobiles and gestured for us to go ahead. VZ and I got in the lift together. I pressed '7'.

'Wow, I'm really loving the way your blue toenail varnish is peeping out of your bobby socks,' he said, looking down at my feet. 'And those shoes are so fucking hot.'

I had on black-and-white striped bobby socks and a pair of black peep-toed heels with ankle straps. I was also wearing a denim pencil skirt, with a clingy black retro batwing top.

'Thanks.'

I thought VZ was being a little over-observant and I laughed. I found his flattery kind of sweet and charming, and pretty harmless. In photos, he was cute. Up close, he looked like a baby, so smooth-skinned, so young. Just looking at him reminded me I was old enough to be his mother. After Kafele, I was through with kindergarteners.

'If I didn't have to do this photo shoot, I'd bend you over in the suite,' he continued.

'Well, somebody already got there first today,' I said. 'Too late.'

'What do you mean?'

'I just had sex before I came to see you with a big black stripper.'

'Really?'

'Yeah, I had an hour to kill,' I said. 'I thought I'd enjoy myself before having to hang out in a hotel with you for the rest of the day.'

He looked astonished that for once someone was telling him to can the charm assault? That cutie-pie rocker wasn't having his way, as usual, with a lady? That his PR woman had shattered the bounds of professionalism by telling him she'd just got laid? That a middle-aged woman had already got more action than he'd seen that day? I wasn't sure which.

We entered the Schiaparelli Suite and greeted the stylist. VZ's manager and agent arrived soon afterwards and made themselves comfortable on the fifteen-foot black-and-beige velvet sofa, smoking cigarettes and admiring the suite. It was half the size of my house. The perfect place for a dirty weekend, I thought, as I brought VZ into the bedroom and secretly admired the super-king-sized bed. Its headboard consisted of a huge patch of black velvet encased in a massive gold-leafed baroque frame, set against a wall covered in hot-pink velvet. The bed was smothered in huge square pillows. Very rock 'n' roll. Though I knew the place had undergone a major facelift, it wasn't quite what I'd expected, given that the Mayfair advertised its 'attractive government rates' for American servicemen. I had a hard time picturing George W. Bush in there, visiting the troops. But it was easy picturing Carl and me on that bed. If only the two of us had killed time here before the rocker showed up, instead of going to tried-and-true Rio's.

'Isn't this fantastic?' I asked. I felt slightly ridiculous, voicing what was blindingly obvious.

'Hey, Fran,' VZ shouted through the door to his manager. 'The next time I'm in London, I wanna stay here.'

'I was worried this might happen,' came a low, female been-there-done-that voice from the other room. She was no fool. The suite was £2,500 a night and, although VZ was a star, he was no Mick Jagger or Bono.

The stylist began to pull clothes out of the bedroom wardrobe and, as I chatted with her, VZ brushed past me, managing to run his hands along my ass. Suddenly his flirtatiousness didn't seem as meaningless as I'd assumed. Does he want me, I wondered, or does he just think he'll get more press by being nice?

'That pencil skirt is so damn sexy,' he said, sotto voce.

'Thanks.' I shrugged.

He moved closer and whispered in my ear, 'Are you wearing any panties under that?'

'Of course not. I never wear knickers.' I looked at him and smiled. Never done a rock star before, I thought.

'Let me take a picture,' he said, and grabbed a disposable camera I'd not noticed before. He handed it to the stylist, a blousy brunette who'd landed this amazing job straight out of college, touring around the world and clothes shopping for the band. 'Jen, will you take a picture of us?'

He moved back to the doorway and pointed to a long glass table in the reception room. 'Here.' He turned to me and said, 'Bend over the table.'

'How did you know?' I said. 'My favourite position.'

VZ got behind me and I pushed my ass into his crotch. I felt his hard-on underneath his trousers. I jiggled my behind and flashed a grin. Click.

Whilst VZ and the crew did the shoot, I took a walk. I wanted to give him a little present, figuring a book with a sexy picture and the words 'erotic memoir' on the cover might whet his appetite. Now I wanted him. I picked up a copy at a nearby Hatchards and returned to the hotel just as the shot was wrapping up. VZ had been moussed, made up and dressed up. He'd exchanged his torn jeans for Prada, put on a black single-breasted Nehru suit over a black shirt, and looked every inch the wealthy well known rocker that he was. And sexy.

'I bought you a present,' I said. 'How should I sign it, to VZ or Vincent?'

'Vince.' He seemed impressed I knew his real name. I'd done my research.

'Wow, that's really sweet,' he said, putting his arms around my waist as I wrote an inscription in the book. I reached for my bag and pulled out my YSL Rouge Pur, applied the lipstick, and kissed page one.

'Something to stop you from getting bored on the plane,' I said, handing it over.

'So, why this book? This ... erotic memoir?' The corner of his mouth curled up.

'Because I wrote it.'

'Think you can you get me some weed?' VZ asked, pulling me aside after the last picture was taken. Everyone was in the suite, getting their things together.

I shrugged.

'We don't really need to stick around, do we?' asked the manager.

'No, it's fine,' I said, hoping I sounded nonchalant. 'I think we're all done here.'

VZ changed back into his torn jeans and crumpled striped Nicole Farhi T-shirt. His manager and agent cleared out soon afterwards, as did the photo crew and stylist.

I picked up the phone. 'Sorry to bother you, Carl, but could you spare a little grass?'

I'm a media whore. I've pimped for a dancer who wanted a date with an attractive journalist who interviewed him. I've served as personal shopper to actors who needed something flash to wear. I've run for macrobiotic snacks for Hollywood directors, and cigarettes for practically everyone. And now I was a drug dealer. There was no end to my talent for pleasing a client.

'Great, Carl, you're a star. You've come through twice today. I owe you,' I said. 'I'll have a bike come round.' I hung up and turned to VZ. 'Shall I hang around and wait for the package?'

'Why don't you sit on the edge of the bed and lift your skirt up instead.'

I smiled and walked over to the bed. I sat down, hitched up my skirt and spread my legs.

He crouched at my feet, pulled my legs up and onto his shoulders, and began lapping my pussy with his tongue. I leaned back, suddenly noticing the open curtains and the view into an office block. 'If people are lucky, we'll give them a show.'

'Mmmmm. Your pussy tastes delicious,' he said. 'So beautiful.'

I let him linger there for a while, tasting me, licking my clit. I enjoyed watching the top of his head.

'Put your fingers inside me,' I said. After a few minutes of having my clit licked and rubbed, I wanted to be filled.

VZ pushed two fingers inside me, moving them back and forth while his tongue licked and sucked on my pussy. My head sank into the fluffy white pillows. I felt myself get wetter and wetter, and I desperately wanted to feel him inside me. That's when I remembered I hadn't brought any condoms. Suddenly, the likelihood of giving him anything more was nil. I had a hard time imagining any rock star sensible enough to pack condoms; it didn't fit the 'live fast, die young' image.

'Come here,' he ordered me, moving away from my crotch and out of the bedroom. I followed, and found him on his knees in front of a 1960s-style chair. It was the shape of an egg sliced in half, hard silver plastic on the outside, hot-pink mock leather on the inside. VZ pushed aside the matching hassock and said, 'Sit on the edge.' I did as ordered, leaning back on my elbows and tilting my pelvis up to give him a better view.

Once again he dived into my pussy, then quickly shifted position to facilitate pushing his fingers in and out of me. I could feel my pussy start to throb and, as it did, VZ pushed harder and faster.

'Get down here, you dirty bitch,' he said, and I obeyed. After all, he was a rock star. I laughed to myself.

I went to lie on the carpet as commanded, but first checked to make sure I hadn't leaked onto the chair. The hotel had only been open a week. Plus, I didn't want to make a mess in a suite I'd scammed for free in exchange for a photo credit. That would have been rude.

A streak of clear oily juices was on the seat. I grabbed a towel from the bathroom and wiped the chair. Then I got down on the floor.

The wool carpet was soft, a brown swirling pattern set off against a biscuit background. Nice to look at, but, I feared, perhaps not ideal for disguising stains. As soon as I felt VZ's fingers re-enter me, and the throbbing resume, I stopped caring.

'Mmmn. This is the spot I was looking for,' he said. He continued to push against my G-spot. I felt the pressure build. I'd never ejaculated before but, as my pussy throbbed, I thought of Carol, a girlfriend from college who, after years under the thumb of New England Puritan repression, had learned to enhance her new life in sleepy Baltimore with violent orgasms.

'Fantastic new boyfriend ... best sex I've ever had ... amazing orgasms ... best lover ever ... makes me gush, and I mean *gush*.'

That last bit got my attention. 'What do you mean, gush?'

'Just resist the temptation to hold back when you're getting fingered. Instead, push, and, Suzanne, I tell you, it'll just happen *naturally*.'

I decided to put her advice to work. As VZ's fingers pushed harder and harder inside me, I pushed against them. It wasn't long before I felt the trickle of liquid between my legs. Getting wet wasn't usually a problem for me, but this was different. It was more like a river, as opposed to the usual drip. When I looked down, there was a puddle of my come on the carpet.

'Wow!' I said. 'That has *never* happened before. I can see the headlines now: ROCKER MADE ME GUSH. Hand me my mobile, will ya? I'll call the *Sun*.'

VZ had already moved off the floor and onto the supersized sofa. 'Lie down,' he said. He stood over me and pulled his cock out of his pants.

My head was just below crotch level. 'Lick my balls,' he demanded, and started wanking. He had a skinny cock, about five inches long and circumcised. Not quite the monster I was used to, not even half the size of the one I'd had earlier in the day. But I wasn't planning on fucking him, not without a condom, so it didn't matter.

I licked VZ's balls whilst he jerked off. He wasn't totally hard, so I nudged my tongue past his balls and began to rim his ass.

'You like that, you dirty bitch?' he said.

'Mmmn,' I moaned. I'd like it a lot more if you had a big hard-on, I thought – you've been watching too much porn, guy.

He put his hands around my throat and gently squeezed. I didn't feel threatened. He was so slight, I could easily have pushed him away had I wanted to. Definitely watches too much porn, I thought.

'Like it rough, slut?' He grabbed my ass and rolled me onto my side. He spanked one buttock hard, then squeezed the flesh. I hoped it wasn't going to leave a mark.

The rough stuff wasn't really my thing, but I thought if that was what it took to get him off, I'd go with it. I'd already had my orgasm and now just wanted to satisfy him. But I wasn't sure I was: he was having trouble staying hard.

The doorbell rang. VZ jumped up, pulled up his trousers, and went to the door. I hid behind an antique Chinese cupboard.

'Sorry, man,' I heard him say. 'Yeah, we're almost finished with the shoot. We'll be gone in twenty minutes.'

'Fuck, I was so close to coming,' he said as he walked back into the bedroom. I reached for his cock and started playing with it.

'I'm really sorry,' he said after a few futile minutes. 'I spent all last night jerking off and watching porn, and I guess I'm all dried up.'

'Don't worry about me,' I said. 'I've had *my* fun. That's the first time I've ever gushed like that. That was quite an achievement.'

'I love coming, too,' he said. 'But I haven't slept for twenty-four hours, so . . .'

He promised he'd make it up to me the next time he was in London. Then he walked into the toilet. 'Come into the bathroom,' he said a minute later.

I got off the bed, pulling off my top and throwing it on the pillows.

'Sit there and play with yourself,' he said, pointing to the toilet.

Charming, I thought.

'Lift your leg so I can see those sexy shoes.' I lifted my leg and rested it on the toilet-roll holder. It wasn't the most comfortable position, and I felt my leg begin to cramp as VZ moved between my legs. He grabbed my breasts. 'You've got amazing tits,' he said. 'Stick your finger in your pussy.'

I did as ordered, feeling more and more like a player in one of his porn movies. He was trying to recreate the scenes but couldn't quite get there in his head, whether from too much booze and coke, a lack of Viagra, or impotence, I wasn't sure. Or perhaps the bullshit didn't fly for him, either. I couldn't help thinking the dirty talk didn't come naturally to him, that it was just part of his rock-star persona, and that in reality he was still the little boy from some hick town in the States.

The door bell rang again, and once more VZ pulled up his pants and went to answer it. 'Yeah … really sorry,' I heard him say. 'We'll be gone in fifteen.'

'We've really got to go,' I said, putting my clothes back on.

'You give great head,' he said.

'That's because I really enjoy it,' I said. 'It's weird, but when I wank, I come while thinking about a guy coming in my mouth.'

'I think about kissing,' he said.

We kissed – our first kiss – and walked out of the room together.

8. ON THE WAGON

I'd grown used to Pat wagging her finger when I described my exploits. She liked hearing about threesomes at Rio's and gang bangs at Torture Garden, yet I suspected, deep down, she was more uptight than she let on. After she sobered up, she got all Catholic on me.

'I just don't understand how you can enjoy casual sex, Suzanne,' she said not infrequently. 'How can you separate the physical from the emotional?' Then she'd ask me for more details about my romps.

She spent day after day on Match.com or MySingleFriend.com trying to find 'The One', and most of her nights at home, alone. She was frustrated and often complained about the lack of available men in London.

One time I gave her the number of a favourite funboy,

Anthony, a handsome cop who used to fuck me from time to time and who was hung and horny. 'He's available,' I said. 'And he's cute. And nice. And he'll fuck you.'

She took his number. They had a chat over the phone, arranged to meet, and then she called it off. A few weeks later, she called again, then cancelled again.

'She's a complete time-waster,' Anthony complained the next time he came over for a playdate.

'Sorry about that,' I said. 'Pat's got a few hang-ups. But she's kinda cute and you would have liked her.'

My buddy Jack had. He was an ex-boyfriend who became pals with Pat after I introduced them during our brief but intense relationship. They shared a love of dogs and took turns looking after each other's pet when one went away on holiday. After our split, Jack would ring me up from time to time, asking if I knew any women who'd sleep with him. I'd hoped he and Pat might pair up but though she adored his terrier, she didn't fancy him.

One day, I had a work meeting in the West End, then popped over to her flat for a cup of tea.

'Almost called you the other day, Pat. I drove by on my way back from the Mayfair,' I said. 'But I was tired and just went home.'

'What was on at the Mayfair?'

'Work. Remember that band I told you about? I fucked the lead singer.' I laughed.

Pat smiled. 'Was he any good?'

'Couldn't get it up. But it wasn't all bad.' I told her how he'd made me gush. She was a gusher herself, and I'd always been a bit envious, because, even though I was the one getting all the action, Pat's party trick had eluded me and made me feel inadequate.

'Anyway,' I continued, 'I'd already come earlier that day, so I didn't need another hard cock.'

Pat's expression darkened. 'You know, Suzanne, two guys in one day, some people might think you're an addict.'

'Are you crazy?'

'It's OK to admit you have a problem.'

'I don't have a problem, Pat. I just enjoy sex. Besides, aside from the occasional lunch-time or breakfast bonk, I only get laid four days a month. Four. Days. A. Month.'

'Well, Jack and I have been talking,' she admitted. Suddenly it struck me that this was something that had been on her mind for some time, and I'd just given her the opener she needed. 'He thinks that some elements of SAA might give you food for thought.'

'What's SAA?'

She went into her bedroom. 'Here.' She handed me a brochure for Sex Addicts Anonymous.

'It's nice to know you're both so concerned about me,' I said, trying not to sound pissed off. I hated when others made assumptions about my motives or behaviour. 'But I'm fine. Really.'

'Just take the brochure, Suzanne,' she said. 'You never know.'

I thought Pat had been judgemental and intrusive, and I wondered what role envy played, however subconsciously, in her purification campaign. I was still fuming a few days later when Karume came by the house.

Ever the hustler, he'd found a new way to pull money out of my wallet. A few months earlier, after he and I had wound down as a couple, I'd discovered that the woman I'd hired to help me around the house had also helped herself to my favourite earrings. Confronted, she stormed out the door in a huff, just in time for my ex to walk back in. Karume was a major fuck-up as a boyfriend, so it was inevitable that I'd fire him from that job. The surprise was that I hired him to be my cleaner right after we split. So he came round every week, dragged a mop around the house a bit, then, if I felt like it, took me up to the bedroom. Usually, as long as there were drinks involved, he was game. He'd mix his special Golden Angel concoction – a big shot of vodka mixed with a little apple and orange juice – if he didn't have a date that night, he'd then slip his cock up my ass and talk my tits off. I'd stopped worrying about his other girlfriends, and he'd stopped asking about my other guys.

Pat hated him because she saw through his hustler act, and he hated her, I suspected, because he knew she saw through his act. And because I'd told him she didn't like anal. I was never sure which one he thought was the bigger crime.

I told Karume about my visit with Pat.

'What were you doing talking to that bitch, anyway?'

'I threw the brochure away,' I continued. 'I could never go without sex. Do you think that's an addiction?' Shit, I just answered my own question.

Karume said no, it was not an addiction, but that a period of celibacy might not be such a bad idea, for either of us.

'What for?' I asked, whilst secretly knowing the answer. I knew what was coming: he didn't want to fuck me any more.

There are three ways a guy dumps his partner: he can say he's fallen in love with someone else; he can move away; or, he can take a vow of celibacy.

'I want to conserve my vital fluids,' Karume explained. 'Think of all that extra energy if I cut out sex for six months. I'll be able to get so much more work done.'

Not housework, I knew. 'What work?' I asked. 'What are you doing now? Other than drinking all the vodka in my freezer, I mean.'

Karume fancied himself an artist these days. He said he was creating a new sound sculpture.

'Six months is a very long time,' I said. 'What about six days? Just as an experiment.'

'I really want to concentrate on my work,' he said. 'Sex is just a distraction.'

'Maybe for you,' I said. 'Not for me. What is it about you guys? When your cock goes up, your brain shuts down? You can still, um, make your art.'

'It would be good for you too, Suzanne.'

'Why?' I asked. 'Sex isn't like drugs or alcohol. It's not harmful.'

'Maybe not harmful, but it can be a distraction,' he said, as he stirred another Golden Angel. 'You'd be more focused if you went without it.'

My prediction came through. Karume's trips up to my bedroom came to an end. He claimed he was giving celibacy a chance, for the sake of his art. But I knew that was total rubbish. He'd begun dropping a new female name into his sentences, kept referring to an artist friend named Kathy, so clearly he'd taken up with someone new.

After his first visit without a sexual pay-off, I thought, Fuck it, why not give it a few weeks, even if he's not. I relished the challenge. And I was keen to silence my critics.

I figured I could still masturbate – as long as there wasn't a real cock involved, that didn't count. And meanwhile I could tone up my vagina with floor exercises. Jahnet, a Maida Vale tantric teacher I'd been to see, had taught me that if I clenched my pelvic floor muscles for fifteen minutes a day, after a month I'd have the tightest pussy in town, and the biggest orgasms, too. And it was true. When I did my exercises regularly, I'd get so tight, I could have scored a job in a Bangkok girlie bar shooting ping-pong balls out of my pussy.

I set my mental alarm for one month's time. Then I called Pat and told her I was giving celibacy a shot. 'I've tried everything else,' I said. 'Why not a month of celibacy?' I realised I wasn't sounding pious enough, and was making it seem like an only slightly more attractive alternative to getting pissed on or having a fist shoved up my ass, two other things I'd not tried before and didn't want to.

'Oh, I think that'll be good for you, Suzanne.'

I cleaned the house, top to bottom. I helped my boys with their homework. I caught up with girlfriends. I kept myself so busy, I hardly had time to think about fucking.

Then, just as deadline approached, I went on a two-week

holiday to India, alone, as my kids were in school and I couldn't find a friend who could take the time off. Arriving in Kerala, I looked around and saw happy, smiley couples everywhere. No unattached men. I was the lone single person at the resort, aside from the waiters and bartenders.

Fortunately, the staffers weren't sexy enough to tempt me out of my dry spell. I was slightly disappointed, as the idea of banging a waiter or bartender was kind of hot, just a dumb fantasy I'd had while packing and thinking of Tom Cruise in *Cocktail*.

I hadn't dated anyone who worked in catering since 1984, when I'd haunted the Soho Brasserie, one of the first cocktail bars in London. I'd go down to Old Compton Street and scam free bottles of Moët from Yan, a bartender my age who, after closing, used to take me back to his West End council flat and fuck me. He was cute and tall and hunky, with a big cock and a tiny brain.

I loved running my fingers through Yan's spiky dark hair, loved looking into his puppy eyes, holding his high cheekbones in my hands. And I loved having his thick hard cock inside me. I can't remember much about our relationship aside from the hangovers, and being underneath him, and drinking the cups of tea that he made on his old upright cooker.

In Kerala I clocked in two hours of Ayurvedic treatments a day, letting myself be pampered by a beautiful eighteen-year-old girl who couldn't speak a word of English. She'd coat me in warm oils, from eyebrow to toenail; walk across my naked body with her tiny feet; sprinkle powders over my skin. The oils and powders smelled bad, but the treatment was the perfect antidote to weeks without sex. Despite being touched so intimately every day, she never got any closer to my pubes than my upper thigh and she circled her palms around, not over, my breasts. She was a tease. It was horny, but I knew an Ayurvedic spa in an Indian resort wasn't likely to offer the kind of 'specials' one can find in the back of a 42nd Street massage parlour. So, back in my hotel room, I made do with the little plastic leopard-print vibrator I'd brought with me from England. It was quiet and didn't take up much room in my bag. And it was efficient, always bringing me to climax in minutes.

When I returned from the trip, I realised six full weeks had passed without any fucking. That was the longest I'd gone without sex, not counting the last four years of my marriage.

I knew I could do it – *ha!* I felt a real sense of accomplishment. I also felt really horny. I called Pat with the news.

'Guess what, I haven't had sex in six weeks! And you thought I couldn't do it.'

'Wow. I'm impressed.' Her tone was cynical. I wondered if she didn't believe me. I decided not to tell her I'd had to masturbate every day to get through it.

During the first month of my celibacy phase, before I left for India, watching men wank on-cam became my second job. Once again, I returned to my one-stop shop for quick cock: Swinging Heaven. I'd found the site a few years earlier whilst searching the web for play partners. It was free, and it always came through for me, so I'd bookmarked the link on my computer.

Not only did I meet a number of guys on Swinging Heaven who'd remained my regulars, some for years, but also it had lots of busy chat rooms. My favourites were the Bi, Bi-Gay, and especially the Bi-Curious ones, because that's where most of the cock shots were and people willing to go on webcam. I didn't want the shy types. I didn't really want to chat, either.

I'd get a little obsessed – if one can be obsessed only a little, be obsessed and not be an addict. Usually, I went straight to the temples of cock, but sometimes, for kicks, I'd go online just to pop into rooms with fun names or amusing activities. Small Gang Bang showed groups of average-looking guys taking turns pounding an overweight woman. Watch Me Fuck My Wife, Big Beautiful Women, Big Black Cock For White Girls –

those rooms had names that said it all, like a *Sun* headline. And then there was Claire's Room.

I heard about it after popping in to my local Borders and running into my friend Marc, who worked at the bookstore. We'd met a year or two earlier, when he'd asked me to come in and sign copies of my first book. A writer on the side, and a perv in the making – I'd corrupted him by telling him about my favourite erotic websites – he appreciated Swinging Heaven because the site gave him plenty of stories to tell. But I got the sense he stopped work on his novel when his fingers started tapping the keyboard.

'Thanks for Swinging Heaven, Suzanne,' he said, sarcastically. 'My girlfriend really loves you for that. She says she never gets to talk to me any more, coz I'm always on the computer.'

That sounded familiar.

'The other day she found me poised over my laptop, fingers at the ready over the keys,' he continued. 'I told her I was playing a computer game, but then she walked over and saw this chat room I had open. I was on Claire's Room – know it? Some gal in Yorkshire sits in a room, stripping.'

'No,' I said, 'but glad to hear something's going on in Yorkshire.'

'It's a game. It's genius. This couple has this chat room, and it's really hard to get into really popular. The woman gets all dolled up in sexy underwear and fuck-me heels, and then her husband asks quiz questions – it's like a pub quiz – and whoever answers right gets to choose what she takes off. She has on, like, ten or twelve items, so it can go on for half an hour. Everyone's at home jerking off and looking up stuff on Google or Wikipedia. It can get quite competitive.'

'I bet,' I said. 'Did you ever get one of the questions?'

'Yeah, just the once, but only because it was about the Sex Pistols.'

'So what'd you have her do?'

'I had her take off this choker-necklace type thing. Not the knickers. That's the last thing off, always after some really hard motherfucker of a question. And then she does a little dance and a tease and slowly peels the knickers off, then the couple fuck on the bed in the corner. And then they do it all over again, sometimes five times a night. Poor sod. Or is it lucky sod?'

'Doesn't it get repetitive after a while?' I asked.

'Not really. Except maybe the music. She always strips to "Man, I Feel Like a Woman" by Shania Twain. Now, I can't watch VH1 Classic any more, in case that song comes on. It'll never be the same.'

Naturally, I went online that night to find Claire's Room. It was exactly as Marc described it. Then I skirted from one room to the next until I found the King's Cross of cock. As usual, it was the Bi-Curious room providing the best action. The straight rooms are filled with women flashing their tits, maybe playing with vibrators or sucking off their partners. That's to be expected – it is, after all, an ostensibly hetero website – but I found it more stimulating to watch one hard disembodied cock after another. Gay, straight or bi, it didn't matter to me – at least not when I was in the cyber world – although I sometimes felt as if I were trespassing. Most of the men in my nightly cock menagerie, I suspected, jerked off for the pleasure of other guys rather than for horny gals like me. Usually, I was the only chick in the room.

Every night during my six dry weeks, I came home from work, cooked dinner and policed my kids, making sure they did their homework and brushed their teeth. Then, whilst they watched a football game before going to bed, I headed upstairs to the loft, home of my virtual sex club, the family PC. I'd flick on the computer, type in my favourite URLs, and prepare for an early evening's entertainment.

I came to know a lot of the guys, or at least their cocks.

Day one of my celibacy countdown, the first guy who caused pause was 'Frank241'.

'You have a beautiful cock,' I wrote, and I meant it. My favourite type is big, thick, hard, uncircumcised and hairless. Just like Frank241's. I decided to stop trolling and stay with him awhile.

He stopped stroking his cock momentarily and moved his hands to the keyboard. 'thx. wot r u in2?'

'I'm into watching men wank,' I replied. 'I hope you don't mind.'

He typed with one hand while carrying on with the other, which took care of any doubts. 'do u hv a cam?'

'No, it broke,' I wrote. Not that I ever knew how to use it in the first place. I could never figure out how to focus the lens, and finally disconnected it. 'You'll have to use your imagination.' I began fingering myself.

His hands, alternating with left and right, continued moving up and down his shaft. Sometimes he used both hands, and I noticed that even with both gripping his cock, one on top of the other around the shaft, the head still poked over the top. His webcam was blurry, the picture froze a lot, and even when it unfroze, everything moved in slow motion. No matter. The quality of the visuals was lousy, but Frank241 made up for it with quantity.

I presumed my alias, SuzyQ, tipped him off that I was a woman, and that he really was bisexual, since he kept private-messaging me. Lots of guys who went on bi and 'curious' sites were gay; it was part of their sex-with-a-straight(ish)-guy fantasy.

From time to time I'd pop a guy's alias into Swinging Heaven's search engine, to check out the man behind the cock. Most of the time they'd listed 'bisexual' next to the S.O. box. 'Married' also tended to be noted. I thought the bi bit was hot; the married part, not. For married guys especially, hanging out in the Bi-Curious room was probably as close as they got to being with another man, and I thought it was sort of sad and pathetic. For me, Swinging Heaven was a temporary diversion from getting the real thing. I'd learned to go out and get what

I wanted a long time ago. Most of these married guys stayed in, jerking off on-cam with guys they'd never meet. In all my years of swinging, I'd never met a married woman who let her husband suck cock.

I debated checking out other boners to see if I could find one that was bigger and harder, but decided to stick with Frank241 until he came. Clearly, he was getting close, as his hands were moving faster and faster and were now focusing on the sensitive tip of his shaft. The blurry cam couldn't keep up. My good deed didn't exactly call for great patience. Thirty seconds later, he came. I could just barely make out the white globs of come, in freeze-frame, as it dripped onto his fingers.

That's one downside of webcams. For someone like me who likes watching eruptions, the climax is anticlimactic. The spunk doesn't exactly shoot out, like in real life, when a cam can only relay a series of static images, like time-lapse photography.

The web had come a long way since I first logged on some seven years earlier, but not the webcam. Towards the end of my marriage, I posted my first personal online. I was looking for a pen pal, not sex, so hadn't asked for a picture. I just wanted someone in whom I could confide my sexual frustrations. I didn't have a digital camera or a scanner then, so wouldn't have been able to upload a pic even if asked. Now, that equipment is mandatory, as are pics, and I wouldn't consider dating a guy who didn't send a cock shot and a full-body pic, or, in a pinch, have a webcam. Many cams continue to transmit out-of-focus images and, coupled with my slow internet connection, they usually leave me wanting more. More than just Frank241 and his big uncircumcised cock. So after he came, I went – back to the chat room.

I knew UKChesterGuy by the colour of his screen. It was orange, which seemed appropriate, as he was large and hairy and reminded me of an orang-utan. He had a beer belly. And man boobs. He didn't show his face. His shirt was always open and hanging down past his gut, so that only a few inches of cock were visible as he wanked underneath it. Which was probably just as well. To me, even a big hard cock does not compensate for a big fat belly. Normally, I would have moved on to a better body, a bigger cock, but I'd checked in on UKChesterGuy just to see what he was wearing. Every time I clicked on, he had on a different Hawaiian shirt, size XXL; he must have had a huge collection. I gave him points for attempting to distinguish himself in a sea of sameness.

That night, a new trick got my attention. Instead of sitting in his chair wanking under his loud Hawaiian shirt, he was standing, giving a side view. His little cock standing out at a ninety-degree angle to his body, UKChesterGuy was bouncing it up and down, up and down, without using his hands. Not just stylish and multi-talented, too. And generous. He was doing his pelvic floor exercises for everyone's benefit, unlike me, who selfishly did it in private. Whilst contracting his muscles to bounce his bits up and down, he was typing: 'Anyone in Cheshire free to suck my cock?'

Not me. I signed on for action. I clicked onto the next name down the list. That was TrannyGirl, who was wearing black hold-up stockings.

There are always at least a couple of guys in the Bi-Curious room who do. The UK is full of fetishists and, if Swinging Heaven is an indicator, then cross-dressing probably tops the list. I gave TrannyGirl points for making an effort. Plus, I had to admit he had good legs, better than mine, so I stuck around.

He was wanking, legs spread, showing the tops of his stockings. I could barely make out something tight, black and PVCish hitched up his thighs. A miniskirt? Probably, as he was wearing ladies' underwear, as well.

He pulled his panties to one side, releasing his cock. I got out my Pocket Rocket, my favourite amongst the dozen or so vibrators in my drawer.

I soon realised that instead of my clit getting twitchy, my thoughts merely turned to Flora, a tranny I'd met at OurPlace4Fun. I'd gone to the North London swinging club a few months earlier, when I was on my own and in the mood to suck some cocks in the grope room. I'd been there so many times, it was like my local, but instead of going for a pint, like most people did at their neighbourhood spot, I went for a pounding or some oral. I enjoyed being alone in that four-by-four dark room, with its familiar holes cut into the walls at crotch level, staring at a line-up of cocks.

I'd been particularly horny that night and had sucked off half-a-dozen guys before returning to the bar to refuel. A 45-ish tranny was sitting next to me, dressed as a firewoman. She was wearing a fitted firefighter's jacket, a tiny firefighter's hat that looked like it came from a children's party shop – it was much too small for an adult's head – plus black fishnet stockings under a pair of black knickers. Her shoulder-length honey-blonde wig spilled out from under the hat.

'You looked like you were enjoying yourself in there,' she said to me, smiling.

I wondered if she was one of the guys I'd sucked off. The room was so dark, all I'd seen were the cocks poking through the walls, not what anyone was wearing.

'Absolutely,' I said. 'Always.'

'I'm Flora.'

'Suzanne,' I said. We kissed on both cheeks. 'So, Flora, what do you do?'

'Ohhhhh,' she cooed. 'I can't tell anyone that.'

'OK.'

We both reached for the peanuts and Chinese crackers on the bar. I thought she was kind of cute and sweet, but not particularly sexy. Transvestism doesn't really turn me on, though the she-male thing does a bit – they get all the best bits. Still, next time I saw Flora, I sucked her dick, just to be nice.

I turned my attention back to TrannyGirl. To my surprise I liked the contrast of the soft panties against the hard-on, the way the transparent fabric revealed the big cock underneath. Like Flora, he definitely wasn't a real girl.

I flicked back to UKChesterGuy. No change there. He was still bouncing his cock up and down and typing into the keyboard, looking for a partner.

I turned back to the menu. Someone tagged BigManMeat had switched on his cam. The name got my attention. Nothing like the direct approach.

I pulled up his profile and a picture of an average-looking, middle-aged white guy came onscreen. He was smoking a cigarette and glancing at the monitor in front of him. He definitely lived up to his tag: a long thick sausage hung down between his hairy legs. Typing a note in the open forum, he was telling BigWilly that his cock looked good enough to suck.

Curious, I pulled up Big Willy's profile. His willy didn't look particularly suckable to me. It was long enough, but thin, and I've always had a preference for long and fat. Not that it mattered; during my austerity phase, I was only window shopping, not buying. Still, I wanted to check out more merchandise, so flicked through a couple more names of guys on-cam.

RP1980 was wearing silky white women's knickers. Done that. UK_Wanker had a skinny white cock and a pale hairy chest. Two strikes. Mashed was naked and had a fit body and a hard cock which looked to be eight or nine inches and quite thick. Bingo. I couldn't see his face, but that was not unusual. Sex sites are pretty focused places, so aiming the cam at the one thing everyone's signed on to see – cock, in my case – makes perfect sense. The cyber sexual smorgasbord gets straight to the point, advertising, upfront, the erotic appeal of everything, from leather, cross-dressing and BDSM to water sports, nipple play, dogging, threesomes … whatever. The straightforward approach is about the only thing about cybersex that is straight.

Mashed didn't show his freckles and dimples and bedroom eyes? Who cared? He showed his big cock, and that's what I wanted to see. I imagined my lips around the head, pulling him into my mouth, teasing his balls. I was getting closer. My vibrator had found my sweet spot.

He reached for his keyboard and typed a private message. 'Hi.'

'Hi,' I typed back. 'I'm watching you wank. Just about to come. Please, don't stop.'

I didn't wait for his reply. I felt my body tremble and I stifled a gasp, knowing my children were downstairs.

9. OFF THE WAGON

Now that I'd silenced my critics, it was time to start making some noise of my own. I'd proven my point, that I could go on the wagon for six weeks and survive the ordeal. Fuck it. Fuck *me*! After six weeks of having nothing but virtual sex, I wanted some real sex – loud, big, messy sex. Hot sex.

Because I'd been so good for so long, I wasn't leaving anything to chance. If I was going to relaunch my sex life, it wasn't going to be vanilla, one-on-one, with just an average-sized penis, especially after all that hot virtual sex, watching kinky, well-hung fantasy men flaunt their mega-meat.

The six-week anniversary came on a Wednesday, but I had to wait two days, until the start of my kids-free weekend, before I could celebrate. Friday night, I ferried the boys to their father's place, then got back in the car and drove over to find some men at Rio's. It was the first sex club I'd ever been to, it was the place where my former partner, Daniel, and I had done our first three-way, and it was the place where I first had sex with my favourite playmate ever, good ol' Greg. So Rio's seemed the perfect venue for popping my post-celibacy cherry.

It was early evening, and Rio's wasn't busy. Weekends are a crap shoot – they're either really busy or really dead, depending on the weather. If it's sunny outside, no one wants to sit in a sauna; if it's cold and damp, everyone does. For a moment, I almost resented the sudden burst of sunny warm weather we'd been having. It was so un-London. It put a real spanner in the works.

I strolled around, didn't see much, so took a nap in the sauna, then strolled around some more. Nothing. I dropped in to the Jacuzzi to kill some more time. Still nothing of interest. I went into the steam room. A guy with a decent-sized cock was in there, but he was already busy, massaging another woman, an anorexic with big fake Victoria Beckham tits. I didn't feel like butting in. It would have been rude, I told myself, to approach two people who hadn't even looked up when a third walked in. Besides, I had to admit, if I were going to do group sex, I wanted two guys, not a guy and a gal.

Clearly, Rio's wasn't going to happen for me that night. I'd hung out for over an hour and seen just a handful of men. Of those, only two caught my eye: massage man, who was off-limits, and a guy who looked a bit like Osama bin Laden, only shorter and lacking the headscarf. He had a decent-sized knob, but when I got a closer look, I saw the hair sprouting from his shoulders and ass and the Prince Albert on his cock. The idea of metal clanging against the back of my throat did not appeal. I left Rio's feeling disappointed, and hornier than ever.

I went back to my car and flicked through the names on my mobile. I texted Greg. 'Free?'

He was – in three days. I debated just driving over to OurPlace4Fun later, after midnight, but didn't want to risk striking out twice. At least Greg was a sure bet. He was hot, always horny and knew how to get me off. And I knew that, as a self-employed carpenter with irregular working hours, he could always make some time to fit me in, or to fit in me.

'Great,' I texted back. 'Monday. Sorted.'

If I were going to get back in the game, this man would help me do it in style. I'd found Greg a few years earlier when I typed the words 'big', 'cock', and 'London' into Google and answered the personal ad that popped up. We became playmates, and got together for one-on-ones or teamed up for sex parties. He could be relied on to stay hard for ages, fuck me in at least six positions and at varying degrees of intensity, and he loved anal.

Fucking me up the ass was a sure-fire way to make me come, especially if I used a bullet vibrator on my clit at the same time. It's the combo of the forbidden and the clitoral stimulation that pushes my buttons.

After six weeks solo, I wanted a thunderous orgasm. Greg's thick nine-inch cock was just the tool for the job, and worth waiting a few more days for. It had a big head that felt great when it entered and stretched me, and balls that fitted nicely in my palm. He liked to dominate and talk dirty, too, which sounded slightly unnatural, and therefore hot, coming out in a middle-class accent. 'Go on, take that cock right inside your mouth,' he'd say. 'The head of my cock is in your ass,' he'd announce, as if I didn't already feel it. Whatever he said, it turned me on.

Greg was nice and smart and amusing, so was fun to be around even when off-duty. He would have made great boyfriend material, too, but he already had a girlfriend. They'd been together for ten years. She wasn't in the game but enjoyed hearing about his exploits. And that made Greg and my get-togethers even hornier, knowing he was providing fodder for sexy stories that would get another girl off. That's the kind of life-partner I'd want – one who got off on hearing my sexy stories and wasn't jealous when I played around.

I went home, made some tea, walked up to the loft and went

online for a wank. There was a message in my inbox, a response to an ad I'd placed on Swinging Heaven months before, when I had been looking for playmates. Most of the responses I'd trashed straight away; others I'd put aside in a folder labelled 'Hopeful', for future reference.

'I am looking for a party buddy,' the message in my inbox said. 'I go to FUN places during the week where you can play 1 on 1 or in a group. If you'd like to link, let me know. To sum it up, I enjoy sex ... friendship would be nice too.'

I liked the message, loved the pics, so tossed him in with the other hopefuls. Then I reread some of the past come-ons, and that got me thinking. Maybe instead of one guy on Monday, I should have three and make this jail break a real ball-breaker.

I wrote to two of the hornier-sounding hopefuls, asking if they were free to meet up on Monday for lunch at Rio's. Both replied with a yes. I texted Greg to ask if he'd mind my scheduling a group thing. It seemed the polite thing to do. I knew it would get him salivating, too. He enjoyed group sex as much as, if not more than, the one-on-ones.

'Go right ahead,' he tapped back.

Just before noon on Monday I received a text message from Greg. 'I have a chest infection. Running a temperature. Feel like shit. So sorry.'

'No problem,' I texted back. 'Feel better.'

I was disappointed. I was also happy I'd made plans with the other two. I learned years ago that men were completely unreliable, even when pussy was on offer. It isn't that they don't want it. It's a scheduling issue. Trying to fit it in between work and other responsibilities, even a sex date with a horn dog can't be guaranteed.

At 12.45 I was walking out the door just as a text came through on my phone. 'I can't be there until 3.' It was HotKnob, one of my two. 'Can you hang around?'

I didn't feel like extending my lunch hour so long and didn't expect my number-three man would, either. If he even showed. He'd not confirmed that morning – a bad sign.

I was beginning to fear my big celebration was devolving into a party for one, no different from the past six weeks.

I went to Rio's anyway. I stepped across the threshold, grabbed my fluffy white towel and made my way to the changing rooms. I was just about to close my locker door when my mobile went off. It was a text from man number three. 'Have to leave town to view a boat I want to buy. Will be in touch soon. xx.'

That seemed an odd excuse, and pretentious. I didn't reply. I put my mobile back in the locker and walked to the steam room.

A couple of familiar faces were already there. One was a guy who was average looking but with a cock that was outstanding, the size of a Coke can. None were play pals, just guys I'd chatted with in the steam room or Jacuzzi on previous visits. They'd been with others at the time, or I had been, and we'd just never connected. If there was nothing going on elsewhere, I figured, one of them would do, perhaps Mr Coke Can. If not all of them.

I walked over to the far side of the steam room and stayed there for a half-hour, alone. I could make out little through the thick of the fog. Then a very tall black guy, about six-foot-five, sat down next to me. He had massive shoulders and the widest chest I'd ever seen. He was completely bald on top, with a trim goatee and a thin moustache. His lips were so large they might have looked comical on a normal-sized face, but like everything else about him that I could see, it wasn't normal sized. Naturally, I wondered if his cock was proportionate.

He squeezed in next to me, and it wasn't long before his fingers began to travel. They moved closer along the tile bench towards me. I felt his fingertips touch my leg. I didn't move away. Soon his fingers inched up my thigh. Again, I didn't move. Emboldened, his fingers marched straight towards my pussy. Still, I pretended not to notice. After a few minutes I opened my legs a crack, and his fingers slid right onto my clit.

That's when he broke the silence. 'I was at Arousal on the weekend. It's a club near Dunstable. Ever been there?'

'No, not tried Dunstable,' I replied. Perhaps not your usual opening, but not so exceptional. People at swinging clubs tend to talk about swinging clubs; they don't talk about the weather as an ice-breaker and, as I'd been reminded by Flora, they certainly don't talk about their careers.

'It's pretty good,' he continued. 'I ended up flaking out at about six a.m. after taking turns on a couple of girls with about six other guys.'

'Sounds fun,' I said. That's exactly what I had in mind when I came here.

'Have you met Nigel?'

How strange. Did this guy think just because I went to a swinging club in London I knew every man in every club in England? I hated to reinforce his presumption, so stayed quiet even though I actually had heard of Nigel, if not met him. He was a legend. Apparently, he was really tall and really skinny, with a ginormous dick. My friend Dawn, a fellow swinging partner of Greg's and the horniest woman I'd ever met, had told me that she'd once met Nigel at Bristol Gardens, a club in Brighton, and had taken his humungous tool up her ass. They attracted quite a crowd, because no one could believe anyone could take in the whole thing.

'Nigel. Black Nigel. Big-cock Nigel,' he continued.

'No,' I said. 'Never met him.'

His fingers rotated inside me. 'He was there,' he continued. 'I thought you might know him.'

'No,' I said. 'But big-cock Nigel. Sounds like I should.'

He was a bit annoying, a bit too big for my liking, and his cock was covered by a towel, so a bit of a mystery, too. I wasn't sure whether to pursue him when he went out the door. But bearing in mind his size and shape, I thought it likely that this huge guy might possess a huge cock. I followed him into the Jacuzzi.

Another chap was already sitting in the pool, in addition to a pair of old ladies comparing bathing caps and ailments. 'Do you mind scooting over, please?' I asked the new guy, smiling, knowing what the answer was going to be. I'd never met a straight man who didn't want a naked woman sitting next to him.

He looked up at me and smiled back, then made enough space so that I could sit beside him. I removed my towel, hung it on hook number nineteen, and climbed naked into the Jacuzzi. The new guy checked me out. I checked him out. Judging from how high he sat in the water, I figured he must have been a little shy of six feet. He had short black hair and was of average build. It was hard to see much, given that most of his body was submerged, but his chest was tight and he looked to be in decent shape. He reminded me of a marine, but I couldn't say why, exactly. He wasn't macho or square jawed or overly muscled, which is my cartoon image of a marine type. But he was rugged looking, had a deep voice, and a tattoo on one arm. Not a marine, but the kind of guy that could get cast in a movie as one.

The black guy was to my right. The three of us began chatting. I told the guys about the three-way I'd tried to set up, pointedly mentioning that it had not panned out. Before either could respond to that info-nugget, four gorgeous black girls walked up. They were all wrapped in towels, their arms holding the cloth close to their bodies. Their presence was unusual. Aside from the ladies over 65, who all wore one-piece swimming costumes and shower caps and used the place as a spa, it was rare to find young sexually available women at Rio's during the daytime. These girls obviously hadn't sussed that the place was a sex club, or, like the older gals, were taking advantage of the £2 entrance fee for women between 11 a.m. and 7 p.m. and were just there to chill out.

The girls all looked like they'd stepped out of a pop video on MTV Base. They were tiny, with the kind of perky tits and smooth skin that can only be found on very young women. Not a hint of cellulite. They were perfect. Each wore underwear under her towel, I noticed, as they stepped into the Jacuzzi. They obviously had never been to Rio's before and, hearing their nervous giggles, I suspected they probably wouldn't be back. For now, though, they were incredibly good value. They kept me and my two mates entertained as we watched them wriggle in and out of the pool whilst trying not to show too much.

'This must be your lucky day, boys,' I said, after the four left the pool. 'I've been coming here for years, and it's the first time I've seen four gorgeous girls all at once, at least before midnight.'

Marine Man turned to me and smiled. 'Did you see the tits on that one?' he said, pointing with a tilt of the head.

'Beautiful,' I agreed, looking over at the girl. 'A combo of youth and good genes. Hard to beat.' She was about a 32B. Her breasts were small and round, with a slight uplift and nice-sized nipples. You better get what you can now, girl, I thought. 'I don't think you'll be seeing any of them here again.'

'No,' Marine Man said, sounding almost forlorn. 'They're not playing. Shame, innit?'

Not for me, I thought. I didn't want the competition. Had those girls been up for fun, my chances of scoring would be zilch.

'I've seen you here before,' said Marine Man. 'Sorry your plans didn't work out today.'

'You're not the only one, believe me,' I said. 'I've been celibate for six weeks, a record for me. That's why I'd planned a little lunch-hour celebration. And now it's been scuppered.'

'Not necessarily,' said Marine Man, smirking.

'I'm sure we could help you out,' chipped in the huge black guy. He'd been so talkative in the steam room, yet so quiet in the Jacuzzi. Perhaps because I'd been stroking his dick under the water, and he was distracted. And it was, as I'd suspected, pretty good sized – as fat as a 300g jar of Bick's Hot Dog Relish.

'Do you really think so?' I said, playing up the coquette, blinking into my neighbours' eyes.

'Yes,' said one.

'I do think we could help,' said the other.

'That's awfully nice of you gentlemen,' I said. I reached down with my left hand and grabbed Marine Man's cock. He was hard. Ah, good ol' Rio's. You'd think that after soaking in a hot tub all afternoon, a guy's cock would shrivel up and go soft. In my experience, they never did.

I did an underwater double-hander, moving my left hand up and down Marine Man's shaft, while feeling the relish jar on my right. Relish Man's cock was so wide, I couldn't get my hand all the way around it. I felt his foreskin slide back and forth over the head. I'm Jewish, and the foreskin thing has always been horny for me. Marine Man's cock was longer but not so fat, with a smallish head that tapered off from a thick shaft. Not as fat a head as I like when it is banging into me, but I'd wanted a three-way celebration and this was not the time to quibble. I took what I could get.

Two hands surreptitiously travelled under the water, one to my left, one to my right. They moved up my legs, then into my pussy, feeling my clit. An old woman in a shower cap stewed in the water across from us, staring into space, oblivious. An Asian gent who'd just popped into the tub sat next to her. Now and then he'd glance in our direction. If he was aware of what going on, he didn't show it. But I figured if I'd felt under the water, it would be clear what was going on in his head.

I felt myself getting wetter and wetter. Giving invisible hand jobs under the water was a turn-on, especially when there was a hard cock in each hand. We carried on talking quietly amongst ourselves, whilst below water we diddled. After ten minutes I'd had enough.

'I really must give you both a blowjob,' I said sweetly.

'I think you really must,' replied Marine Man.

'I think that's essential, don't you?' added Relish Man.

We all stepped out of the Jacuzzi, the men grabbing their towels to cover their erections so as not to spook the Grandmas, and together walked to the back of the club, where there were two rooms reserved for group activity. The 'relaxation rooms' upstairs were earmarked for couples only and were off-limits to threesomes and absolutely a no-go for crowds. In all my years going there, I still hadn't quite worked out why Rio's made the distinction. My theory was that the rule made policing easier for the management. Sometimes, I had to admit, it was hard to tell whether a lone man was stalking a couple for had been invited to join up and was just following at a discreet distance. It was a hassle shooing away single men who made pests of themselves or who didn't respect boundaries.

Thc three of us stepped into one of the group rooms and closed the door. I didn't feel like giving a show or attracting another player. I'd come for two men and now I had two men.

I laid my towel on the gym mat that padded the platform and got on my knees. The play mat was the size of a single bed, but a clever trio could finesse the space. The boys removed their towels and stood facing me, cocks aimed at my mouth. I grabbed the white one first, sucking the narrow head, my right hand moving up and down the shaft whilst my left stroked the black cock.

'Fuck, that's a big cock!' said Marine Man, looking over at his neighbour. And he was right. The thing was much bigger than it had seemed underwater – not long, no more than six inches at most, but incredibly fat. It may well have been the fattest cock I've ever seen, and I've seen hundreds. I can't be absolutely certain of its status, but at the time it seemed a record-breaker.

'All the girls say that,' said Relish Man. The two guys laughed.

I sucked and sucked, alternating between the long narrow white cock and the short fat black one. Stroking off one whilst licking and sucking the other, I closed my eyes, enjoying having a cock in my mouth and another in hand. I heard the men moaning.

'Ahhh,' said one. 'Suck that big cock,' said another.

I felt pressure at the back of my head, someone pushing my mouth deeper onto the black cock. It was hard to get much of him into my mouth, although I didn't mind that. I was happy to work for it, and I wanted him to enjoy the experience as much as I was.

As I moved back on to the white guy's cock, I heard muffled noises coming from the rest area on the other side of the door. I figured we had probably attracted a small crowd, thanks to the spitting and sucking and moaning noises we were making. It never took long for word to travel through the club when a group thing was in the works. And apparently, as usual, all the men had bolted in the direction of the sex sounds, assuming they were invited. I was happy I'd locked our door.

I moved onto the platform and got on all fours.

'There's some condoms in my bag,' I said. As ever, I'd brought along my kitbag, filled with the necessities: condoms, lube, butt plug, and vibrator, plus shampoo and conditioner for afterwards.

Relish Man handed me a condom.

Marine Man knelt in front of me and slipped his cock back in my mouth. I felt Relish Man trying to enter me. He pushed hard, pushed hard again, then again. After some difficulty, he was inside me, his cock straining the walls of my vagina, forcing me wider as he made his way inside. He thrust hard and opened me up but, unlike my regular morning man, Sam, he wasn't long enough to hit the tip. Still, it was delicious, feeling filled up after six weeks of running on empty.

There was a knock on the door.

'Can I come in?' said a male voice. 'I've brought some drinks.'

Marine Man looked at me, while his cock pointed to the ceiling. His expression seemed to indicate that if I took the drinks now, I'd be taking something else in a minute, as well. I looked again at his towering cock. Go for it, Suzanne, go cock crazy, I thought. It's been six long weeks, you deserve it. I thought of Jennifer Aniston and her L'Oreal commercials: 'Because I'm worth it.'

Marine Man opened the door a crack. A guy in a towel was standing there, holding three glasses of something. He was cute, a white guy about five-foot-ten, in his late thirties, with a toned body that looked to be completely shaved.

I was thirsty. 'What the hell,' I said.

Marine Man opened the door all the way and tilted his head to the side. 'Come in.'

'Take your towel off, mate,' said Relish Man. 'She doesn't want to see your towel. She wants to see your cock.'

That was true.

He removed his towel. I saw that his cock was already hard. It was average, about six inches long. The new guy helpfully held a glass to my lips. Lemonade. Lovely. Most of it slid down my chest, and I laughed.

'Fuck me up the ass,' I said.

'What a woman!' he replied. 'Triple penetration for lunch.'

What, is this your first time? I wondered.

I heard the foil rip open as he removed a condom from my bag. Relish Man was fucking my vagina from below, Marine Man was in my mouth. I felt a third cock probe my asshole. 'Go slow,' I warned the newbie. 'I'll lead.'

He pushed in hard and it hurt.

'Stop!' I shouted. He obviously hadn't had much experience with anal, not knowing he had to start off slowly. He pulled out quickly.

'Wait!' I said. Definitely inexperienced. You don't push in fast, you don't pull out fast either.

'I'll tell you when to push again,' I said. 'And put on some more lube.'

I felt my sphincter relax after a minute. 'Now,' I said. 'Slowly.'

But it was too late. Maybe it was the small play mat that made it tough for four players. Maybe Lemonade Man didn't really want anal. Maybe he just didn't know how to *do* anal. Maybe he didn't want to hurt me again. Maybe he didn't like being so close to another guy's cock. The two guys' cocks were probably rubbing against each other. Not every man's cup of tea. Some guys just don't like coming in contact with another guy's equipment, and that makes double penetration complicated in group settings. It takes two experienced guys to really get it right. Hence, the appeal of experienced swingers like Greg.

I couldn't tell if it was me who'd wrecked the moment, or twinges of homophobia in Lemonade Man's head that fucked it up, but whatever it was, it didn't work. When Lemonade Man tried sticking it in once more, his cock went soft. I waved him over, and he came round to my side, cock in hand. I reached towards it and began stroking.

The room was hot. Everyone was dripping with sweat. I slid from one cock to another, and the energy built between the four of us. The men took turns in different positions. Relish Man reclaimed his original place and pounded me from behind. Marine Man gripped my head as he pushed deeper and deeper down my throat. He took turns with Lemonade Man, whose cock I graciously bobbed up and down on, bringing him back to life.

'She's so fucking sexy,' I heard one guy say.

'Beautiful body,' said another.

I was desperate for something to drink and desperate to come, but the two agendas were in conflict. Despite all the physical activity and the stimulation and the energy and the pheromones running through my body, I could not orgasm. I thought back to the sex I used to have with Karume, how we'd pace ourselves, build up to the threshold of an orgasm, then slow down before quickening the pace and beginning all over again. In the group room, it was all about excitement, about the now. There was no slow, no gentle. The focus was on hard cocks, willing pussy and deep-throat blowjobs.

I wanted to take a break. I asked for something to drink. Relish Man left the room to take care of it. Lemonade Man made his exit too. Now, it was just me and my marine.

'Thank God,' I said. 'That was getting a bit much.'

He laughed.

'Can I grind on your cock?' I asked.

He smirked.

'That's what I'd really, really like to do,' I added for his benefit. Now that the others were gone, I could concentrate and come and be done with it.

'Sure,' he said. 'Use me, treat me like a dildo. Do whatever you want with me.' There was not a hint of irony in his voice.

He got down on the mat and lay on his back. I straddled his hips. I pulled him deep into me and felt my clitoris make contact with his pubic bone. He was hard inside my pussy. We were still soaking with sweat.

I closed my eyes, concentrated on the sensations, and continued grinding, grinding. I relaxed into his hips as my clit rubbed against him. It felt nice being with a man after six weeks without one, felt nice going one on one after the frenzied group activity of the past hour.

The door opened again and Relish Man walked back in with more lemonade. I gulped down the glass gratefully. My body began shaking, perhaps from the sudden sugar jolt after all the energy I'd expended, perhaps from the mixture of sexual excitement and adrenalin and relief at being done with abstinence, forever. I felt like the pocket vibrator in my bag, switched to low, as the jolt subsided to a gentle hum inside me.

I looked up, and there was that black cock again, hard and thick. I was close to coming and, as my mouth took hold of it, I suddenly found it difficult to concentrate on sucking while my orgasm was building. I pulled away and watched Relish Man wank. Then I came. Gripping Marine Man's shoulders, I pulled myself hard into him, as the waves of contractions shot through me. My juices dripped all the way down his cock.

I climbed off and, knowing Marine Man still hadn't come, started to jerk him off. Karume always said my handjobs were impossible to resist, and I wondered if perhaps he was right because, two minutes later, I felt Marine Man get harder, and then, putting my mouth round his cock, felt the come shoot out of the end.

'Oh!' he screamed. 'Goooooood!'

I looked over at the big black cock. 'I don't want to come just now,' said Relish Man. 'I'll save it for something hotter.'

We all laughed.

A few minutes later, I was back in the Jacuzzi, chilling with Lemonade Man and a guy named Leo, whom I'd fucked once before. Or rather, tried to, till we both realised that, with his two-inch cock, oral was better. And thankfully he knew that without having to be told.

'Was that you making all that noise back there?' Leo asked, snickering.

'Yes, afraid so,' I admitted. 'Sorry, didn't realise we were so loud.'

He reached over and touched my shoulder. 'You don't fancy a massage, do you?'

'No, honey, I'm outta here in ten minutes,' I said, remembering the last 'massage' he'd given me, a few months earlier. I didn't fancy going back there in a hurry. The oral was great but the cock was not. 'Another time, perhaps? Really, I have to get home.'

I'd had my end-of-celibacy celebration, got what I'd wanted, and now I had just a few minutes to take a quick shower and change before picking up my kids from school. Within half an hour I was standing outside the school gates waiting for my children, a smile on my face.

I wondered why anyone would champion celibacy. Pat may have thought I was a sex addict, but after my afternoon threesome, I came to the conclusion she was just jealous.

10. ON THE ROAD

I pulled my mobile out of my bag and scrolled through the numbers for someone who lived nearby. John! I tapped a message. 'You free for the next hour or so?'

An answer came back a minute later. 'Yeah. Why.'

'Flight delayed. At Heathrow Terminal 3. Time to kill. Wanna meet?' A blizzard had blanketed New York and all flights in were cancelled. They rebooked me on a later flight, but it wasn't leaving for six hours.

'Got 1+ hr. Be in front 20 mins. Can't wait to taste yr pussy.'

Twenty minutes later, John pulled up in front of Terminal 3 in a shiny new black Range Rover. Aside from the extra stone he'd acquired around his middle, he looked about the same as when I'd last seen him, two years earlier – still bald, blue eyed and handsome. I assumed his cock was still seven inches and fully functional.

'What happened to the taxi?' I asked.

'Oh, I'm semi-retired now,' he said whilst picking up my suitcases and flinging them into the boot, just as his former cohorts were doing for others at the taxis lined up beside us. 'I started investing in property, and now I've got a little portfolio.'

No small accomplishment in the brutal British market, where just getting in on a refurb is a huge hurdle. I was impressed.

'It keeps me busy,' he continued, 'and it's a bloody helluva lot easier than picking up drunks at night and ferrying them home.'

I thought of the times cabbies had driven me home in that same condition. But John wasn't one of them. We'd just used his cab for sex.

'Travelodge?' he asked.

'Perfect.'

I leaned across the seat to kiss him on the mouth. Nice. So were the leather seats, which were wide and comfortable, quite a trade up from the days when I used to crouch down in the back of his TX II, sucking his cock.

'Nice to see you again, John. It's been too long.'

'Yes, it has.' He smiled as he drove. 'I'm really looking forward to this.'

So was I. He was as horny as hell, and loved having me grind on top – my favourite position. He could stay hard for hours, provided I sucked him between orgasms – that was his favourite thing. He loved licking pussy. What was there not to like?

Ten minutes later John pulled the Rover into the Heathrow Travelodge car park. The motel was nondescript but convenient, used mainly by business people who needed something near the airport for an overnighter before catching an early flight out.

We walked in through the front door and up to reception.

The cute blonde girl behind the desk, perky and efficient, asked for a credit-card deposit and a photo ID, and had us fill out a form with our names and addresses. The process took ten long minutes, biting into our time. No wonder we used to fuck in the taxi, I thought, tapping my foot in irritation.

I pondered the ridiculousness of all the bureaucracy, given we'd be in and out of the Travelodge within an hour. The company sure wasn't exploiting its profit potential. It could have jacked its margins by creating a FasTrack system for illicit encounters like ours. We just wanted a quickie, a literal fuck 'n' fly. Thinking like a madam, I was calculating the cash flow of a room being turned over for people like us 24 times in a day. I was beginning to wonder if I'd gone into the wrong business.

'How many rooms have you got in this hotel?' I asked the receptionist.

'One hundred and sixty-five. And you're in Room one hundred and seventeen,' she said, handing John the key and gesturing. 'The lift's over on your left.'

We walked to the lift and kissed as soon as the doors closed. I felt John get hard as our lips met.

'Mmm,' I said, touching his erection through his jeans. 'That didn't take long.'

We continued kissing as we exited into the first-floor hallway and all the way to Room 117. We entered the room, kissed while removing our clothes, and got naked on the double bed. I lay on my side and took John's hard cock in my mouth.

'That feels great, Suzanne,' he said. I felt him go from hard to harder.

I sat up and swung my legs over his, until my pussy was directly above his cock.

'I'm sorry,' I said, all come-hither. 'But I really must fuck you right now. I'm soooo sorry.'

'Go right ahead,' he said, smirking. 'I want to feel you grind on this cock.'

He gripped his cock and held it against my pussy. I moved my pelvis up and down, teasing the head of his penis.

'Does that feel good?' I asked.

'Fan. Tastic.'

'Good.' I ground down on him and pushed against his pelvic bone. 'Because I'm going ... to come ... soon.'

I shut my eyes and carried on, grinding down on his cock, feeling him hard inside me. Even though I hadn't seen John in a long time, fucking him felt familiar and comfortable.

That's the way it's always been with me and my lovers. Very few men I've had sex with seem to go away forever, unless they've gotten married or fallen into a serious relationship. The rest, the majority, reappear at some point, taking up with me again after weeks, months, even years, when in the mood for a reunion or after stumbling upon my number while going through their little black book. Then, reunited, our comfort level is no different than it would have been had we seen each other the day before. Sexually, the action tends to remain fresh and fun. And I like it that way. I built my stable of studs around one goal: avoiding the monotonous and the stale.

I bounced on John's seven inches for ten minutes or so, then came, groaning loudly. John came with me. He reached for me, pulled me close, and together we laughed at the movie moment. Simultaneous orgasms may be a Hollywood cliché, but there's something magical about them nonetheless. Looking into a partner's eyes, teamed together as the tension mounts, the double head rush adds an extra degree of intimacy to a sex act.

'Not bad, John!' I said. 'I haven't done *that* in a while.'

'Or me,' he said.

'You mean *I* haven't done *you* in a while, or you haven't had a simultaneous orgasm with someone in a while? Which is it, boy?'

'Both ... girl.' He smiled.

He held me in his arms till his cock softened. Then I rolled onto my side. It felt nice to cuddle, like being with an old friend.

'So, what you been up to?' he asked. 'Still fucking around?'

'Same old, same old,' I said. 'Yeah, still fucking around. And writing about it!' I told him about my book and its being my reason for being at Heathrow in the first place.

'Sorry, I forgot you'd been writing,' he said. 'I never picked it up. Should I have done?'

'Well, you're being immortalised. If only in one paragraph.' I described his appearance in the book: the taxi driver who shot his load so often and so heavily, I had to change condoms every few rounds, when one became too full of spunk. 'I should have called you the heavy repeater.'

He laughed. 'I guess I'm gonna have to go buy it now, huh,' he said, raising an eyebrow, 'as I've got such a great write-up. Thanks.'

'You're welcome. Now go capitalise on the PR and get some pussy,' I said. 'So, what about you, what's going on?'

'I've had a couple of girlfriends,' he said. 'Nothing too serious. The thing is, I really want a kid, but I really enjoy the whole swinging thing, too.'

'Can't blame ya,' I said. 'Swinging's great. Kids are great, too. A lot more work, though. And easier with a partner.' That, I knew firsthand. Even when I was married to a man who spent more time at the office than at home, at some point along the way, there was an extra set of hands if needed.

'I'm not sure I could ever give this up,' John continued. 'But there's a part of me that really wants a relationship. Don't you ever want to settle down, Suzanne?'

I shrugged my shoulders. John wasn't the first person to ask me if I wanted to settle down. 'Don't you want a boyfriend?' was a question I had heard almost every day for the past five years, ever since getting divorced. I'd learned to live with it. Most people assumed that, because I didn't have a boyfriend, I wasn't complete. To me, it wasn't a matter of wanting, or not wanting, a boyfriend. I'd simply stopped looking, stopped thinking about it. If it happened, it happened.

This is an alien approach to life, apparently. Women's magazines are always giving top-ten tips for finding or keeping a man; girlfriends are always calling up, worrying about losing one guy or strategising to score another; romance novels always end with an HEA, the happy-ever-after ending, which really just means the girl gets the guy; Hollywood makes a fortune off perpetuating a rosy view of romance that doesn't exist in real life. We're bombarded with shit telling us that monogamy is the be-all and end-all and that settling down is the ultimate goal.

But I'd already ticked the boxes on most girls' life plan – the children, the job, the car, the home – and was getting good, steady sex on top of it all. Now, I was in a position to concentrate on pleasure. While most women don't even get laid, or settle for a token fifteen minutes once a week, I'd found a group of people who didn't think that was good enough. Getting good sex was one of their top priorities and, like me, they took pleasure in giving pleasure. If that meant not conforming to society's pro-monogamy propaganda, fuck 'em.

I understood the need for companionship. And I understood the desperation of single women like Pat, who knew that, until they got a partner, besides not getting laid regularly, they'd probably not have enough money to raise children on their own or buy their dream house. So they paced the floor every night, frustrated and panicked and alone, watching the clock. For a while after my marriage, I subscribed to the idea that a new relationship would make me happy, but a few years on, I wised up and realised I was happier on my own.

'I'm not bothered being alone,' I said. 'What's the point? Maybe this'll sound a bit wacky, but my psychic –'

John raised an eyebrow.

I met his gaze. 'Yes, my psychic – she told me there's someone out there for me, and I believe her.' I explained that even if

Morene had not made that prediction, I'd have come to that realisation on my own. I'd always believed that one day someone would come into my life, someone who got me.

'That means, no secrets,' I said. 'I know the swinging thing freaks the average guy out, but I'm not looking for average.' I stared down at his cock. 'Obviously.'

We laughed.

'Face it,' I continued. 'It's not easy, especially with the kid thing in the background. But that doesn't mean you can't find something special and lasting. I've met plenty of people who've made it work.' I described some people I knew who were in committed relationships but were far from monogamous. 'But until it happens for me, I'm not going to waste my time worrying about finding someone who understands it.'

This was getting serious. Fun boys don't want serious. I changed the subject. 'So John, want me to suck you off one last time before we drive back to the airport?'

'Why not?' he said, grabbing his cock and shaking it like a toy.

I bent over him and once more took him between my lips. Moving my mouth quickly up and down the shaft, I sucked it back to life. He came within minutes. I sucked the come into my mouth. Then I cleaned off the head of his penis with my lips.

'That was nice, but I'm exhausted now,' he said. 'I wish we both didn't have to go.'

'Me, too,' I said, standing up. 'But we do have to go. Shall we?'

I grabbed my clothes off the floor, dressed, then suddenly realising we hadn't bothered to get under the covers, I adjusted the bedspread. One less room for the housekeeper to clean. It gave me a little thrill to think about what we'd done without leaving any evidence. It was like trespassing or having a secret.

John pulled up in front of the departures area, kissed me on the lips, then got out of the Rover and put my suitcases on the pavement, ever the full-service taxi driver.

'Thanks. Don't be a stranger, John.'

'I won't,' he promised. 'Let's get together when you're back.'

I walked through the revolving door and into Terminal 3 feeling both light-headed and damp between my legs, a sensation that only happens when I've been properly fucked. I was already flying.

11. THREE IS NOT A CROWD

I never wanted to be famous. Given the drawbacks, fame just did not seem worth it.

Working with celebrities in my job with an entertainment company, I knew the price they paid just for existing. Sure, their lifestyle seemed glam: massive money and multiple houses, first-class travel and expensive designer sunglasses. Their fame attracted as many flashbulbs as invitations to yachts in Monte Carlo, villas on Lake Como or ski lodges in Gstaad and Aspen. It meant non-stop interruptions, whether it be calls from agents and personal assistants or requests for endorsements and autographs. It meant never being alone. Paparazzi stalked, hangers-on hovered, pimps and dealers procured, and most human interactions meant being recognised and treated like an object. I'd stumbled drunk out of nightclubs plenty of times in my life, but never had to face seeing my picture in the tabloids the next morning, documenting the experience.

As far as I could tell, the only good part about being a celeb, other than the wealth and the luxury, was the endless freebies. No designer gives free couture, cars and carats to an anonymous author, alas. But when I published my first book a few nice things came my way.

I got offers of one-handed massages from more than one guy who envisioned rubbing me down with one greasy hand while stroking his cock with the other. I got invitations to lunches at the Great Eastern Room and Oxo Tower from guys who wanted a private dessert at a handy hotel afterwards. I got calls from journalists who offered column inches in their newspapers and precious minutes on their shows. A middle-aged mother who went to sex clubs and orgies, had one-night stands and powder-room quickies with strangers, I was, if not exactly a celebrity, infamous, even under a pseudonym. If people didn't want my ass, then they wanted my time.

A trip to New York to promote my book showed me the upside of notoriety.

I hadn't lived there since I was thirteen, nor spent any time there alone since breaking off my long-distance relationship with Frank five years earlier. After we stopped seeing each other, there wasn't much reason to go back. I no longer had family in the city, and friends I wanted to see preferred visiting me in London. To my mind, New York had lost its edge anyway, since Mayor Rudy Giuliani had shut down the sex shops and backroom bars starting in the mid-1990s, and 'redeveloped' Times Square by plunking glass office towers where strip clubs had once been. It had become a family destination, replete with Disney Stores and Madame Tussaud's. New York no longer seemed the place to swing.

But when the *Howard Stern Show* came calling, I took the opportunity to give the city another chance. Stern wanted to talk – about my colourful sex life and, secondarily, my book – so I booked a flight and began planning my trip, as well as some saucy outfits.

Stepping out of JFK, I was immediately assaulted by a blast of freezing air. Suddenly, I appreciated the hideous down coat that Karume had given me the previous spring. It was a present that showed up the day after my birthday, which is to say, one day after I'd grumbled about not receiving a present from him. Normally, I don't care about gifts, but it pissed me off to have been forgotten by someone I'd supported the previous twelve months. Though no longer even boyfriend and girlfriend at that point, we slept together from time to time, while I continued to pay for his wardrobe, dinners and vacations full-time.

He'd given me a black bomber puffa jacket, something I was unlikely ever to wear, except in a pinch, as when travelling into tit-crunching sub-zero temps. An unlikely thing for me to wear, all right, as Karume no doubt knew. I favoured slimline clothing – tailored coats, pencil skirts – and never dressed all wrapped up, layer over layer, like a piece of baklava.

I assumed Karume had nicked the jacket, either from the wardrobe of one of his secret girlfriends, or from a clearance rack somewhere, as opposed to actually buying the thing. He never had any money.

'This is an interesting present,' I'd said, hoping for a clue.

'I thought it would keep you warm.'

I never did find out where it came from, but had to admit he'd been right. It was warm.

It also made me feel safe, I quickly discovered. On the SuperShuttle ride from the airport to my Greenwich Village guest house, I got tossed around in the passenger seat as soon as we picked up speed on the expressway. Not the kind of action I preferred in a vehicle. WTF? I looked over at the driver and noticed the guy was barely looking at the road. Instead, he kept looking down at the clipboard on his lap. Not the usual aggressive New York driver, a dime-a-dozen horn-honking road pest, this guy was a burly Eastern European lug who either didn't know how to drive well or couldn't be bothered to follow the rules. He kept looking down at the clipboard, scribbling notes no matter the traffic or speed, while careening from one lane to the next, over icy roads, never signalling, refusing to take the pen out of his hand or his eyes off his clipboard.

Clearly, the guy was nuts. I gripped the handle on the door, both to calm my nerves and to prevent myself from getting tossed out of my seat. After a while, I'd had enough.

'Excuse me,' I said, 'but is it necessary for you to take notes while you're driving?'

'Yes, is necessary,' he said. Firmly. Not looking up. End of enquiry.

That shut me up. I felt slight comfort knowing the big ugly puffa jacket provided a lot of padding, putting a few layers between my body and whatever it seemed destined to crash into.

The next day promised a soothing antidote to the terror ride of the night before. I was invited to high tea on the elegant Upper East Side.

A woman named Viviane had proposed a tea party in my honour. She called it the Perverts' Saloon Tea Party, a monthly gathering of sex bloggers and writers. My timing was perfect.

'My out-of-town guest is Suzanne Portnoy, who will be making several appearances in connection with her book, *The Butcher, the Baker, the Candlestick Maker*,' said her invite. 'We are also honoured because Sissy Maid Stephanie will again be serving us.' I didn't get that last reference, but appreciated the plug and looked forward to an event that promised fun with some fellow travellers.

I'd met Viviane online a few months earlier, around the time my book came out in the UK, when I was researching the swinging scene in America and wondering if anyone there would buy a dirty little book like mine. I'd been told that

Americans didn't read erotic memoirs, that the country's puritan streak ran straight across the map, as it were, from coast to coast. I was dubious. I'd met pervs from San Francisco to Boston, Chicago to New Orleans, covering all points on the compass, so figured that, despite George Bush's sex-negative laws and prissy Oval Office proclamations, a sexual underground had to be burbling just under the asphalt of Main Street, USA. Every action has a reaction; nothing like repression to start a scene where there wasn't one before. I'd been taught my Newton in college, but had also learned first-hand while there, in that small New England town, that drugs and three-ways, orgies and tea-room blowjobs all existed. They just weren't pictured on the postcard.

Viviane was a major mentor of American sex bloggers, the networking queen of the genre. Most bloggers linked to Viviane's Sex Carnival or referenced it, and no wonder. She was a jackpot for news of interest to sex-positive communities, vice law info', health tips, and erotica, all with a sprinkling of kinky pix.

I put on my blue-denim pencil skirt and black keep-you-warm tights and, thanks to the Arctic blast, my trusty puffa. Then I took the subway uptown.

In the lobby of Viviane's elegant apartment building, I took off my coat as the doorman buzzed me up. One minute later I was in a roomful of New York pervs, who entertained me with their stories of the city's swinging and sex-party scenes. It was a relief to know Giuliani had not banished all the fun from Gotham.

A middle-aged man in a wig and a pink French maid's uniform walked around the room serving tea and nibbles. 'Thanks, cheers,' I said, as he dropped a lump of sugar in my tea. 'Are you Stephanie?'

'Sissy Maid Stephanie,' she said clarifying. She was heavy set, talked with a deep New York accent and performed her duties with relish.

'I used to teach school,' she told me later, as we walked down the street towards the garage where she'd parked her Oldsmobile Cutlass. Sissy was still in costume, and though she got a few looks and smirks, the New Yorkers carried on with their lives and left the sissy maid to her own. 'I retired a few months ago. This is sort of my new job, when I want to "work".'

On her way back to New Jersey Stephanie dropped me off at the guest house. I was feeling a little tipsy, having knocked back a couple of glasses of bourbon after Viviane brought out a bottle for the party's stragglers. A little jet-lagged, a little sleepy after a fitful night in an unfamiliar bed, I felt my head spin. Then I began feeling juiced up.

I made a booty call to a guy I'd found on Craigslist a few days before leaving London. I had posted an ad seeking a dancing partner, though dancing wasn't really what I'd had in mind.

'Sexy erotic authoress coming to New York to launch her book,' I'd written. 'Seeks a fit, handsome, chocolate-coloured partner to accompany me to a NYC hotspot for dancing and debauchery sometime next week.' The first person who wrote back fit the bill.

We'd arranged to meet and go dancing later in the week, but suddenly I wanted to see him now.

'Hi,' I said, laying on the British accent to jog his memory. 'It's Suzanne.'

'Hi,' he said. 'Daniel. Nice to hear from you. Where are you?'

'The Village. You wanna meet up?'

'Could be there in a half-hour,' he said.

'Great. Meet you on the corner of Eighth and Jane?'

Thirty minutes later, there he was. Black, about six feet tall and slim, buzzed on top, with a goatee below, he was just my type. He looked at me approvingly as I approached. I returned the look. Then we moved towards each other and kissed in a way that is more intimate than usual for two people who don't know each other.

'Whadya wanna do?' he asked in a TV-show New York accent. 'Wanna drink or something?'

'No, it's too late,' I said. 'Why don't we just go upstairs? I'm staying three doors down.' I pointed to the door of the Incentra.

'Cool.'

Together we walked up the hallway stairs, Daniel grabbing my ass from behind. I heard a clock strike nine or ten or eleven times; it seemed to bang on forever. Daniel pushed my skirt up over my waist as I shut and locked my door. I took off my boots and tights and inched over to the bed and lay back. He put his head between my legs. By the time the clock chimed again, Daniel had fucked and sucked me and gone out the door. Welcome to NYC, Suzanne, I said to myself. Thank God for Craigslist.

The next morning, I was up by six. I curled my hair and put on an outfit I'd had made especially for the *Howard Stern Show*, even though I knew it was unlikely anyone would see me in it.

Stern is a man worth going to New York for. His show is notorious in the States, as much for its scatological humour as for its riffs on conservative politicians with little cocks that matched their little minds. That, and the ritual request Stern made of his female guests, whether Hollywood starlets or rockers or porn stars, that they lift their tops. Stern started out as a disc jockey in a Boston suburb, then got a drive-time show in Hartford, eventually ending up in New York and becoming America's highest-paid shock jock, as well as the one most frequently fined by the government's dirty-talk police. Now he had a $500 million gig on Sirius, a national audience of millions and had expanded to TV. The television show was an edited-down, weekly-highlights version of the daily radio programme. With that, along with the porn stars' balloon-sized tits, in mind, I figured I and my 46-year-old, slightly sagging boobs would not make the cut.

Nevertheless, I wanted to look my best, even for a radio slot.

I dressed black and tight – houndstooth blazer, matching pencil skirt, fishnets and sky-high KG heels. I put on my glasses, looked in the mirror and thought, I could be mistaken for a librarian. A sexy librarian, but still a librarian. Poor gals, no one ever thought librarians got laid. But I'd met a few on the circuit who proved life wasn't all about the Dewey Decimal System.

The show went better than I'd expected. Howard was kind and funny and reasonably polite, playing the schoolboy whose education hadn't included the slang words for penis, vagina and anus throughout my 25-minute interview. But a dirty-minded schoolboy just the same.

'Have you licked a man's anus?' he asked.

'You mean rim, Howard, don't you?' I said. 'I think we can use the proper expression for it.'

'I didn't realise there was a proper expression for it,' he said.

I laughed. I was sitting opposite a man who tabloids linked to scores of porn stars, and even if that was just PR, he certainly knew what rimming was.

'Yes,' I replied. 'I've rimmed a few asses.'

Then it was time for the listener phone-in.

Stern: 'Irish John, you're on the air.'

Irish John: 'Hey, Suzanne baby, what you doing? Wanna go see Blade at B.B. Kings?

Me: 'Well, I'd love to, but I'm going to do a reading tonight at the Happy Ending lounge.'

Howard: 'How you going to do a reading with Irish John's cock in your mouth?'

Me: 'It will be hard. I'll mumble through it.'

After the show I went back to the guest house, threw off my clothes, climbed into bed and napped for a couple of hours. Then my phone rang. It was Tim, my college sweetheart, the guy who'd dumped me for my pal Marsha during our last term. He hadn't called me in 24 years, but I'd kept track of him and, prior to my visit, had emailed everyone I knew in New

York, including him, for the hell of it, and given my contact info.

Tim had heard me on Stern, his idol. 'You were amazing,' he said. 'Cool and calm. I couldn't believe how great you sounded.'

'Thanks,' I said. 'It was fun. Thanks for calling.' I wondered if he regretted dumping me all those years back.

'I'm really proud of you, Suzanne.'

I turned over and went back to sleep.

When I woke up later that afternoon, I put my hair back in curlers, reapplied my make-up and dressed for my reading at Happy Ending. It's a former erotic-massage parlour on the Lower East Side, that has been given a second life as a swinging-1960s-style cocktail lounge on one floor. It retains the tiled shower stalls and sauna from its last incarnation, with tables and chairs and mood lighting added, turning the basement into a warren of cosy booths. Its website actually advertises an 'intimate, almost indecent atmosphere that harks back to a pre-Giuliani New York' – a bit forced, perhaps, but the blurb serves as confirmation that Giuliani's crackdown was a feat of historic proportions.

I wore my 'lucky dress' – the leopard-print halter-neck number that I'd first worn at the Erotic Awards. Since meeting Carl, the Rump Shaker, my first night in it, the dress had become my fail-safe pulling outfit. It showed off my curves and, when I was squeezed into a black push-up bra first, it gave me the lift I needed. A fashion stylist had once told me during a shoot for a soul-singing diva, 'Foundation garments are everything,' and, judging from my ongoing successes in the outfit, she was right.

I arrived at Happy Ending half an hour before the show started and was met by a guy named Greg. He had written to me after reading a piece about my book on the *Sunday Times* website, and we'd corresponded since then. He hadn't offered any sexual favours; he just seemed like a normal, nice guy, who wanted to know where he could pick up a copy of my book.

He was about my age, a bit short of five-foot-ten, medium build, with a small goatee, short dark hair swept up in spikes, brown eyes that glistened in the club lights. I took inventory and found him just as cute in person as he was on his MySpace page. We hit it off instantly. He was sharp and funny and sweet and, as we chatted in the corner booth at the far end of the lounge, I found myself thinking I had to add 'sexy' to my list of adjectives. He worked as a film editor. I thought that was cool. And he lived in Greenwich Village. I thought that was convenient.

'I'm staying in the Village,' I said.

'That's handy,' he said, smiling.

I topped the bill that night, and I revelled in the attention that resulted. The space was narrow and dimly lit and packed full of people of all ages, all types. Standing centre stage before fans who had read my blog or heard me on Stern that morning, I enjoyed sharing excerpts from my first book, and digressing before the appreciative crowd to ad lib anecdotes. It was a reminder of just how much I enjoyed performing for an audience, something I'd done only sexually in recent years. I had briefly considered a career in theatre while at university, but chucked the idea when I realised I was good at stealing scenes but not good enough to star. Standing in front of the microphone at Happy Ending, I felt like one.

Full of adrenalin, I stepped off the stage and walked over to Viviane, who had brought along some fellow bloggers to see me.

'Hey!' I said. 'So good to see you again.'

She told me I'd been great, invited me to a little Vietnamese place around the corner for dinner, then introduced me to the dark studious-looking man next to her. Very tall, very slim, twenty-something, he was wearing tiny round wire-rimmed specs and a preppy Ralph Lauren polo. He looked like a world-weary college student or a tortured poet, very much the humanities-studies type.

'Hi,' I said.

'Hi,' he replied. 'Flint.' His voice was soft and low, like an American DJ on a jazz station. It was a strange name, but I remembered hearing it before. The previous evening, after describing some of my conquests over a cup of tea, I heard Viviane say to someone, 'Don't you think she'd like Flint?' I later found out Flint wasn't his real name. His real name was a conglomeration of unintelligible Nigerian syllables few Americans could get their tongues around, and he'd given himself a cooler-sounding alternative shortly after arriving in the States to attend NYU.

'So, wanna join us?' said Viviane.

'Sounds great. I'm starving,' I said, giving Flint another up-and-down. 'Let me go and grab my friend.'

The restaurant was a cavernous fluorescent-lit space filled with huge, round Formica tables that sat ten. A lazy Susan was in the centre of every table, each filled with soy sauce, condiments and plastic chopsticks. Mirror tiles and posters of cranes and Chinese bridges decorated the walls. It was only 10.30, but we were the only people there and, between the unflattering light and the desolate atmosphere, it seemed about the least romantic spot in all of downtown. Fortunately, Greg and I had already quaffed a few Manhattans at Happy Endings, and with two cuties at my table, the promise of another happy ending was on the docket.

'Beer or wine?' Viviane polled the group.

I voted for beer. Viviane called over the waiter and ordered Singhas and food for four. I was tired and a little tipsy, and it was nice to let someone else take charge. I sat between Viviane and Greg, with Flint opposite, which gave me the chance to take him in.

'Have you read Flint's blog?' asked Viviane.

I confessed I had not. I'd not even heard of it. 'He's a really good writer,' she continued. Viviane was a warm and generous woman. I was grateful and flattered that she had come to my reading and then invited me to join her for dinner.

We closed the restaurant an hour later. Viviane looked at

her watch. 'I have work tomorrow. I really should make a move.'

'Soho House, boys?' I said.

'Are you a member?' asked Greg.

I looked at him, raised a brow, said nothing.

'Oh, wait!' he said, suddenly remembering the many scenes I'd described in my first book that took place in the toilets of the club's London branch. 'Of course you are.'

'What's Soho House?' said Flint.

'Meatpacking District club,' I said. 'C'mon, let's get a nightcap.'

We packed Viviane into a taxi, then Greg flagged one down for the rest of us. I sat between Flint and Greg. 'Two handsome men and me. It doesn't get more perfect than this.'

Greg put his hand between my legs and kissed me. His mouth was soft and warm. As his hand travelled up my leg, I whispered in his ear, 'Rip my tights.'

I felt his fingernails dig into the nylon, but the material would not give way. I'd bought cold-weather tights especially for the trip, and they proved very protective indeed. They were indestructible.

'This is a lot harder than you think,' he said with a laugh.

'Try harder then,' I said.

He dug his nails in deeper and pulled and pulled until eventually the material tore open, giving him just enough room to manoeuvre his fingers towards my pussy.

'Thank God,' I said. 'I thought you were never going to get there.'

Greg's index finger pushed to open me, making me instantly wet. Then Flint put his hand on my thigh and inched up. By the time we reached Soho House, their fingers were lubricated from knuckle to fingertip.

We stumbled out of the cab, past the bouncers and through the front door. 'C'mon, c'mon!' I laughed, leading the guys to the lift.

It was midnight and the sixth floor was packed, as the

London club always was, with media people and models, most of them, as in London, drunk. We took a seat at the far end of the leather banquette. 'Manhattans, guys?'

'Why not,' they said.

We had just the one round. My mouth moved from Greg to Flint, Flint to Greg as we sipped, exchanged kisses, sipped. I liked the contrast between the two men. Greg, my age and experienced; Flint, young and keen.

'I think we should leave now,' I said after we emptied our glasses. 'Let's go back to my place. There's a bottle of wine with our name on it and a few beers in my fridge.'

Fifteen minutes later we were in the guest house rearranging the furniture with our bodies.

Greg pulled over an armchair and sat on it, stroking his cock. I stood in front of him, my legs shoulder-width apart, naked aside from my ripped tights, heels and push-up bra. I watched him masturbate for a minute. Then I bent over, took his thick six-inch cock in my right hand and began sucking him off.

Flint was behind me. I felt his hand reach between my legs and, yanking on my tights, he probed my pussy with his cock. It was thick and very long. His cock hit the top of my cervix when it slid in its full length.

'That's incredibly hot,' said Greg as he watched my head bob up and down. I took his almost painfully wide cock in my mouth.

'Isn't it,' responded Flint. He was sliding in and out of me, pushing against my cervix, making me wetter and wetter with each thrust.

I grabbed the arms of the chair as Greg pulled my head in close, easing my mouth down onto his cock again and again to take him in.

Despite the number of drinks we'd all consumed, the guys were rock hard and my mind remained clear, as focused as an accountant on the numbers. One, two, three inches ... six. Greg must have been as thick as he was long.

I loved thinking about having these two big cocks all to myself, and about being desired by two attractive men.

'Why don't you fuck Flint while I watch?' said Greg.

Flint pulled out and moved himself onto the double bed. Lying on his back, his long body took up the full length of the bed, head against the headboard, toes dangling over the other end. His cock stood straight up and, seeing it for the first time, I wondered how I had managed to get all of it inside me. He was as long as the rulers we used to use at school, and a hell of a lot thicker. It was a real fucking cock.

I climbed over Flint and eased myself down on to him. As I moved my body slowly up and down his cock, I felt him get harder.

'Wow,' said Greg, 'that's a big cock!' I felt his eyes boring into my back, watching me ride Flint.

'Very big,' I said, moaning. 'Very. Maybe a little bit too big. But it feels amazing.'

'You don't mind if I just watch, do you?' asked Greg. 'I'm pretty wrecked.'

I looked behind me and saw Greg had his cock in his hand and was wanking listlessly.

'No,' I said. 'Of course, I don't mind.'

'Your pussy is so wet,' said Flint. His hands were now on either side of my waist, lifting me off his cock and then down again.

'And your cock is so big,' I said. 'I don't think I've ever had a cock so large before.' It was a porn cock, like something from BlackOnWhite.com.

'I know,' he said, proudly. 'Sometimes I think it's almost too big. Some girls don't like it.'

'Well, I'm not one of those girls.'

'I noticed,' he said. We laughed.

I heard rustling in the background and turned to see Greg pulling on his jeans and shirt. 'I'm gonna leave you guys to it,' he said. 'I've gotta be up early for work, and I've been burning the candle at both ends a little too much.'

I climbed off Flint and went over to Greg to kiss him goodnight. 'I'll call you,' I said. At Happy Endings we'd made plans to have dinner in a couple of days.

'Have a good time, you guys,' he said, smiling, and walked out the door.

I turned around and looked at the bed. There was blood on the bedlinen.

'I'm really sorry,' I said, surveying the crime scene. 'I didn't realise it was that bad. I thought I was at the end of my period.'

Flint laughed. 'Doesn't bother me.'

I climbed back on his cock and continued grinding down on him, moaning as I did so. A short while later, Flint passed out. I followed close behind. Neither of us came.

When I woke up at dawn to go to the toilet, I could not understand why I wasn't able to get around the bed to my destination. Somehow the bed had become wedged next to the armchair and created a barrier. I had to climb over Flint, who was still comatose and splayed across the mattress. It wasn't until I came back into the room that I realised our romp had completely altered the design of the room. The bed, normally up against the wall midpoint between door and window, had moved three feet to the side, and was in the centre of the room. I crawled back onto the mattress, put my arms around Flint, and went back to sleep. I woke up two hours later, when I felt Flint's hard dick against my buttocks. I climbed on and, as usual when I have morning sex, came quickly. So did Flint.

'I should go,' he said at 8.30. 'I need to get to school.'

School? I thought. I've just fucked a guy young enough to be my son!

Even though young guys tend not to be my thing, though now and then I end up with one. But never before had one used the word 'school' during our time together. I hoped he meant grad school.

Not bad, though, for a middle-aged broad.

I kissed Flint goodbye and went back to sleep.

12. A NOSH WITH A POSH

I didn't think of myself as the next Virginia Woolf, didn't expect my book to bring me a Whitbread award or an invitation to appear on *Richard & Judy*. But I did feel that sex-positive messages, whether mine or anybody else's, were practically a public service to the frowning masses, home or abroad. Promoting my book in America seemed almost like a contribution to the greater good. And getting laid while I was there was a bonus.

When I returned home to London, I was on a high. It had felt great to be appreciated in New York, both as a sex writer and as a sex object. But now it was back to relative anonymity, to being a player on the London swinging circuit but no longer showing my face around town as the author of an erotic memoir.

Back to normal life. For me, that meant back online.

I found in my inbox a message from a dating site called Flirtnik, offering me a free month's membership. I receive solicitations from dating services almost daily, but then I had been on pretty much every dating and 'dating' website around the world for years, so no doubt am probably on hundreds of mailing lists, with an asterisk next to my name indicating 'sure bet'. Flirtnik's email caught my eye because it reminded me of Nerve.com, the first erotic site I'd ever visited. Nerve featured fiction, photography, film and book reviews, and blogs, all about sex – plus personals, to float the site. It was New York-centric but somehow kind of poncey, with the air of a Gap ad. Everyone on it looked naturally attractive and a bit too wholesome. It was sexy and had gotten me laid, a lot, in the past, but I'd moved on to lower-tech, but more hard-core sites, and hadn't looked at Nerve for three years.

Flirtnik aped the look but not the flavour of Nerve. It was pure vanilla. Still, it was free, and I'm Jewish, so I posted my profile and had a look around the site. There were five men in their forties listed. One was called Honest Jim. He hadn't posted a picture but, valuing honesty, particularly after my adventures with Karume, I thought this guy might prove refreshing. Equally intriguing, Honest Jim's profile said he worked in the music industry and, being in the entertainment business myself, I thought that was a plus. I sent him a wink.

A day later, I got a message back. 'So, after my first tentative steps into the brave new world of cyberspace, I already have a response. That is so cool. Flirtnik is a shite name, don't you think?'

I knew then he had potential.

We exchanged pics and sent long emails back and forth every day for a week. I recalled my own first steps into cyberspace, five years earlier, and enjoyed playing the seasoned traveller to Jim's newbie. He was cute enough, despite some very crooked teeth, and he had a huge variety of interests, mentioning English literature, music, gallery shows and football matches all in the same email, and not sounding like a pretentious wanker. After three days I found myself looking forward to opening up my inbox to see if there was a message from my new buddy.

I knew from our correspondence that he had always been monogamous, and had never done the swinging thing or been to a fetish club. He seemed like just a normal nice guy, a real change from some of the men I'd been hanging out with. I wasn't looking for a boyfriend, but I had thought I'd found a friend in Jim and possibly a new fuck buddy too.

Then, seven days into our chatfest, Honest Jim confessed that his ex had come back into his life. And being that rare monogamous type, he said he thought it only fair to break things off before things started. I found that a bit presumptuous. We hadn't even met, much less slept together. All he'd done was send me his pic and a few emails, and although he wasn't unattractive, he was certainly no George Clooney.

I confessed to being slightly disappointed that we never hooked up, but I'd survive. That's the way things go in cyberspace. Honest Jim went back to his girlfriend. I went back to my fuck buddies. And shortly afterwards Flirtnik went out of business.

Since my first Swinging Heaven hook-up with Sam, we'd arranged our schedules for a meeting time that worked for both of us. Every two or three weeks he'd come by for a breakfast that did not include cereal. I'd drop my kids off at school at 8.45, then turn around to get back home for a nine-o'clocker. Sam was always on time.

He'd ring the bell, come in, and fuck me until I came. Then I'd suck and wank him off, and we'd go. We soon got to know each other's preferences so well that most mornings I'd be at work by ten and he'd make his regular 9.45 Friday staff meeting, conveniently just up the road. Our sessions were as much about efficiency as speed. He knew what to do to get me off, and could do it quickly.

'Can I come and fuck you senseless in the morning?' would be a typical Thursday-evening text.

'Yes.' My typical response.

One time he came to the house, marched me up to my bedroom and fucked me without saying a word. I played along. After that, words weren't necessary. I'd get a text the night before setting out the morning's agenda.

'Will text you when I'm outside,' said one message in my inbox. 'I want you to open door, go upstairs and wait on the bed. Legs spread wide open, rubbing your cunt for me. Wear a blindfold. X'

'Naked or lingerie?' I asked.

'Lingerie,' he replied, so lingerie it was.

'And your wet pussy will be all mine. Going to fuck you hard and deep, make you come and then leave you in the blindfold. Leave your toys out.'

No meet was ever the same, and each got slightly kinkier than the last. I suspected Sam took pride in concocting new scenarios for us to play out.

'I want to come up the stairs and be watching you two-finger fuck yourself for me. Get me hard and ready to slide my thick cock inside you. Your pussy better be ready.'

His wish was my command.

'God, I'm hard,' he texted another Thursday night. 'God, I love fucking you.'

'I'm going to shave my pussy for you NOW,' I wrote back.

'Just what I like – a nice, wet, shaved, ready pussy. No fingering without me tonight. That's all mine.'

'OK.'

'Get it all finger-fucked wet and spread wide open for me. My mouth will give you all you need. Caress my head while I lick you out.'

As became our ritual, the next morning I did as instructed and lay on my bed, wearing a pair of skimpy red lacy boy-shorts, a black bra, and my favourite high black patent fuck-me shoes over flowery red bobby socks.

Sam fucked me in every position over time – often blindfolded, start to finish – until I'd come, sometimes in bed, sometimes bent over and gripping my kilim-covered easychair with one hand, massaging my clit with the other. He would ease his big cock in and out of my ass or pussy. After my contractions eased off, he'd take my hand and turned me around, sitting me up in bed or down on the chair. I'd take his cock in my mouth while he stroked the shaft. A few minutes later, I'd feel his warm spunk on my lips, tongue and face. I'd leave on my blindfold, then listen for the footsteps. He'd slam the door shut and be gone in thirty seconds.

One afternoon, I met a guy the old-fashioned way: in person.

I was at High Road House, a members' club newly opened in Chiswick, for Sunday brunch with my girlfriend Bernadette. We had known each other for fifteen years, but hadn't seen each other in six months, as she lived on one side of the Thames and I on the other. We spoke regularly, but somehow London geography got in our way. A catch-up was overdue.

Following the hostess to our table, we walked in the direction of a handsome grey-haired gentleman. He looked to be in his late fifties, and was sitting with three other people about his age, two men and a woman. Bernadette and I were seated in a corner by the window, a perfect vantage point for surveying the people in the room and, happily, right next to Handsome Man's four-top. I looked over at my neighbour perhaps a bit too frequently, but he met my eyes frequently enough, so when it came time to leave, it seemed only logical to slip my card to the maître d'.

'Would you mind giving this to that distinguished older gentleman at that table by the corner?' I asked him, trying to sound nonchalant.

For a moment the maître d' looked taken aback, but he quickly collected himself, then offered to oblige. I didn't linger to see if he was true to his word.

At 6.30 that evening I received a voice message on my mobile.

'I was extremely chuffed and delighted to receive your card,' said a guy who sounded like Prince Philip, 'although I have absolutely no idea who you are.' He said his name was Max and gave his number. 'I must say, I was sufficiently intrigued by your boldness to invite you for a drink.'

Even though I'd heard only snippets of the conversation at Handsome Man's table, I could have sworn the man I wanted was an American. Max's posh accent didn't gel with my memories.

Still, I called him back. 'Listen, before this goes any further, can I ask you something?' I said. 'You were the guy who was sitting with two men and a woman on Sunday, weren't you?'

'No,' he said, sounding rather sad. 'I was sitting with a man who is much older. He is a judge.'

'Right.' I said. 'Sorry, Max, you're not the guy I thought you were. We might as well end this conversation right now. But thank you for calling.'

'Please,' he said, his tone almost pleading. 'Please. Don't go. You sound absolutely delightful. Just meet me for one drink.'

I pondered. 'So, what do you look like?' I asked.

He said he was about six feet tall, medium build, grey haired and 54 years old. 'And in quite good physical shape,' he added.

'I'm not usually into older guys,' I admitted.

'Oh, just the one drink, Suzanne. I promise, if we get along, I'll buy you dinner. Then if that works out, I'll buy you a car. And after that, a house. I have a million pounds in my current account.'

That made me laugh, and since his deep baritone was alluring – I've always had a thing for deep voices – I accepted. Max and I worked out a date two weeks in the future, as my diary was full until then and, in the period leading up to our dinner, we talked on the phone almost daily and got along well.

I called Bernadette to update her on post-brunch developments.

'Can't you even *try* to like him?' she asked. 'It sounds like he ticks at least some of your boxes – car, house, loads of money.'

'I'm trying to keep an open mind,' I said. 'Really.'

'Good. I think this one sounds like he could be The One.'

'The One' was a bit of a joke between the two of us. Morene, my psychic, had said there was someone out there for me when I'd last seen her. She'd predicted that I was going to meet a man much older than I, a guy who invested in creative companies, lived on a mews and 'collected things'. She said that if I didn't dismiss him for the usual reasons I tossed off men – small cock, beady eyes, tiny ears, wrong shoes – I'd end up marrying the guy.

Max seemed worth a shot.

He turned out to be pleasant-looking and pleasant to be around. He was quite a gentleman, too, but not the distinguished gent I'd stared at over brunch. Though his face was a little too pink and round for my liking, as I prefer thin and angular men, he had a surprisingly handsome profile. Dressed in a navy-blue-blazer and chinos – rather conservative for my taste – he looked like an umpire on a cricket field. But he was a great storyteller and loved drinking, so the champagne went down well as Max told funny stories about his days in advertising and about his friends, whose names were straight out of 'Jennifer's Diary' in *Harper's*.

I found myself fantasising that his having a million was true. Just the idea of all that money made me moist. Most of my men lived off their overdrafts.

Max invited me to stick around for dinner. A good sign. He was still telling stories when I looked at my watch. It was midnight; four hours had dashed by, and I'd hardly noticed. I began to wonder if Max could grow on me, despite my not being overly attracted to him. Certainly, financially he was a far better prospect than any of my previous boyfriends, ever. And unlike so many monosyllabic types I'd put up with in my youth, he was a great raconteur. He really knew how to spin a yarn, and for a change that took the pressure off me. I'd always fallen into the role of court jester, so it was a mini vacation to be able to sit back and watch someone else hog the limelight.

After that first chaste date, we carried on chatting on our

mobiles daily. He would entertain me with stories about recent dinner parties at aristos' stately homes, and then turn to other current events in his life: mostly battles with his social-climbing ex-wife and problems with his spoilt teenage daughter.

I called my friend Janie, a long-time single with a penchant for unavailable married men, and told her that for once I'd met a guy with a car and a job and a million pounds in his bank account.

'Wow,' Janie said, 'maybe he's The One.'

'Oh, I don't think so,' I said. 'I'm just not feeling it.' I told her how even on my first date with Rump Shaker, I'd felt something. 'Even if it was mostly in my loins and a lump in my throat.' I explained that I felt a lot more comfortable around Rump Shaker, that with him I didn't have to prove anything. And that I always wanted to see him again. Though Max was entertaining, I didn't feel any great urge to see him a second time.

'Let me get this straight,' she said. 'You're telling me that you'd actually prefer being with a human strippergram with diamonds in his teeth, no permanent employment, four kids from three different mums *and* financial problems, to an extremely wealthy, smart *and* attractive, single older man?'

'Yeah. Stupid, eh?'

'Don't you want, like, a real guy?' Janie said. 'At least one with long-term prospects?'

'Right now? Actually, no,' I said. 'I'm just having too much fun at the moment.'

'You're nuts,' said Janie, laughing as she signed off.

I thought it interesting that my girlfriends had such different takes on the men in my life. When I'd told Pat that Rump Shaker had a second career as a builder, and that he sometimes did handiwork around my house, naked, taking his tea breaks in me, she thought he could be a contender.

'What about going out with him?' she said. 'He seems like he has real potential: builder, sexy, big cock. He sounds right up your street.'

Just as I hung up from Janie, my phone rang. It was my

human strippergram, calling to say hello and to tell me how work went the night before. We'd spent a few hours together earlier that day, when he'd come round to fix a leaky tap, then he'd gone off to perform at three hen nights in a row. He collapsed into bed with one of his exes at four the next morning, he said.

To most girls, that call would have been a reality check, but it just made me laugh. I'd never considered Rump Shaker boyfriend material, and I didn't mind that he slept with other women or that his life was a bit complicated. I knew I'd see him again, when the time was right for some mutual fun, and that was enough.

About two weeks into our tête-à-tête relationship, Max invited me over for Sunday lunch at his house in West London. The prize on the menu was pheasant, which he boasted of shooting a few days earlier on the estate of some titled friends. Between the twin lures of roast pheasant and society gossip, he had me.

The bird turned out to be a bit dry, but after sharing two bottles of Margaux, I wasn't exactly parched.

'I've been thinking,' Max said suddenly, 'that our first break should be a weekend trip to Chicago.' He asked what my schedule was like.

I told him, for starters, that I couldn't get away that easily. I had two kids in school and, unlike his monied-up friends, no domestics to pick up the slack. As for my two kids-free weekends coming up that month, they were booked already.

It was time I made clear I was not looking for a serious boyfriend.

'But wouldn't you *like* a serious boyfriend?' Max asked.

'Not really, not right now,' I said. 'I'm having fun just juggling.'

'Well, *I* don't do the "crash and burn", dahling,' he said. 'I want an *adult* relationship. Do you know what that means?'

I thought I did, but I knew he was going to tell me anyway. Our conversations were strictly one-way affairs. He talked, I listened. And listened and listened. I wouldn't have, normally, had he and his boarding-school accent not been so amusing.

'I don't mind your dalliances, Suzanne,' Max said. 'Just don't make me jealous.'

His words surprised me. Apparently he had decided on a relationship without consulting me. This is a first, I thought.

'Clarify your intentions,' I said.

'I'm not interested in having more babies, or in our doing the laundry together. And we can't be platonic,' he said. 'I just want someone with whom I can spend the weekend, preferably away. That means nice holidays, nice hotels . . .'

'Sounds perfect,' I said, and I meant it. It did sound perfect. Except there was one small problem: I wasn't sure whether I fancied my meal ticket.

Max opened a third bottle of Margaux and suggested we 'move upstairs'.

I held a glass of wine in one hand and gripped the railing with the other, as Max took my arm and led me up the stairs. We walked into his bedroom and I almost tripped on the books and clothing that littered the floor. I saw eyeglasses, pills, more books, old newspapers, an overflowing ashtray and cufflinks. And that was just the side table. This wasn't organised chaos; nothing looked intentionally placed, like in a design magazine. This was just a mess, and it wasn't romantic.

Max kissed me hard in the doorway, then began ripping off his clothes, contributing new piles to the floor. Almost immediately we were on the bed having sex. There wasn't much foreplay, not even much kissing. He just rolled me over and tried taking me from behind, doggie style.

I crouched, at his request, on all fours, and stared at the patterns on the grey-and-black duvet cover.

'Could you please tilt your bottom up just a little bit higher?' Max asked, ever so politely.

I complied.

'Just a few inches more?'

Again, I complied, arching my back like a cat. I got the sense he wasn't hugely experienced. He didn't know how to give me any pleasure, and didn't seem particularly interested in offering any. If he had been with a lot women, it certainly didn't show as, sooner or later, one of them would have taught him the golden rule of good sex: ladies first.

Although I'd had a porn-star fantasy for years, this wasn't the one. In my brain, I was with a hot black guy with a ruler-length dick while a Richard Gere lookalike shouted do-this, do-that directions from the sidelines. Here was a 54-year-old white man with a skinny five-incher asking me, politely, what to do, but instead of fulfilling my fantasy, he was just making me work.

After about a half-hour in the cat position, it hurt, and not in a good way. The skin on my elbows felt raw after too much time in one position. Too much time, because Max couldn't keep it up.

'Would you like me to take a Viagra?' he asked once the obstacle to our lovemaking became clear to both of us.

'Yeah, sure.' I tried to sound game, though I really wanted to go. The throbbing elbows were a painful reminder of their existence. Usually, I spent my time in bed pursuing pleasure, not feeling pain.

'I'm really sorry,' said Max. 'I normally have no problem getting hard.'

I mumbled the usual assurances.

'I find you a bit intimidating, to be honest,' he confessed, before taking a stab at a joke. 'I'm sure I can't be the first man to say that!'

'You're not.'

I was reminded of Tom, an edgy actor-comedian who'd told me the same thing not so long before. We'd met through business, and after our work meeting he'd invited me out to dinner. We flirted through appetizers and the main course, but put our pudding off. A few days later, we booked a cheap North London B & B for some lunch-time fun. But despite his own reputation, he found mine harder to handle.

He'd picked up my book after meeting me and quickly caught on to my big-cock fetish. He'd boasted about his size over dinner, but that was before reading about some of the men I'd been with. Too late, he realised his cock wasn't that spectacular after all.

I spent most of that afternoon stroking Tom's cock whilst stroking his ego. I sucked his perfectly fine above-average cock to keep him hard enough to fuck me in the short bursts before more tongue action was required. A sweaty 45 minutes later, we both managed to climax, but it was one of the more challenging sessions I'd ever had.

Until I met Max, that is.

The Viagra didn't do the trick.

'I really must go,' I said, after giving the Viagra the requisite twenty minutes to kick in. I explained that I needed to collect my children from their father's house. My kids-free weekend was over, as was my affair with a 54-year-old toff. When I heard the front door close behind me, I felt relief. The feeling surprised me, but I could not deny its message.

I rang Max the next day to tell him I didn't want to see him again.

'I just don't think it's going to work out,' I said. 'I thought it best to just tell you before, you know . . .' Before you book any weekend trips to Chicago, is what I wanted to say.

'Oh, I feel quite forlorn, Suzanne,' said Max. 'I was just going to ring you up to tell you how much I liked you.' He said nothing about our sexual non-experience.

The omission brought to mind my experience fucking Oliver, a film director two years Max's junior. He was another private-school-educated guy with a posh voice who didn't make me come and hadn't seem bothered. I'd found him sexy on the street but a bust in bed. So focused on the goal of coming, he forgot that was my goal, too.

Although I could see the attraction that came with the older-guy package – power, confidence, money – I'd yet to meet an older man with whom I felt a real connection. I wondered if, having achieved a certain status, they'd grown selfish and didn't care about their partner's pleasure. Or maybe they'd just never learned the basics, having slept with women who never opened their mouths to express their needs. I didn't understand how a guy could pass the half-century mark and not have figured it out.

Perhaps I was doing something wrong; perhaps it was my fault I didn't click with these guys. I called my friend Paula. A gorgeous 38-year-old singer with long brown hair, sexy Germanic features and a slim curvy body, she could have had her pick. And she picked as her husband a man in his mid-sixties. After he died, she took up with a 62-year-old.

'What do you see in these older guys?' I asked her.

'They just seem to know what to do,' she said. 'They're more sensuous, more loving. Sex isn't about a race for them.'

Easy for her to say. In my experience, just getting to the starting line was an accomplishment.

13. PLEASURE AND PAIN

'Paul came by today,' Pat said one day when I popped over for a cup of tea. 'Remember him? Cute, Scottish guy, skinny?' I recognised the name instantly, even without the description.

I'd first seen him two years earlier at a birthday party for Pat. He'd stuck in my brain ever since, unlike Max, who flew out of my head about as quickly as he'd landed there.

Pat's party was held at Guanabara, a Brazilian club in Covent Garden, and the place was so full of hip young Latinos swivelling their hips and wiggling their asses, I felt like a foreigner who had accidentally landed in Rio de Janeiro.

I'd just gone blonde again and, middle-aged to boot, knew fitting in would be a challenge, so I'd worn a long black ruched skirt that looked vaguely Spanish, with a tight red top knotted around my midriff. I couldn't be Latina but I could do sexy.

And I did feel sexy as Jack spun me round on the dance floor and kissed me between songs. That didn't stop me noticing Paul, though. He stood out because he was another fair Anglo in a sea of dark-haired hotties, and because he was my type – lanky and undernourished looking, with high cheekbones and short blond hair just beginning to go grey. He was about six-feet tall, with broad shoulders and narrow hips, and had the kind of human-hanger body that made anything he wore look good. He was wearing a 1940s-style double-breasted blue suit with a flat cap and brogues. He was arty and handsome and carried himself with the confident air of an original.

'Who's the guy in the cap?' I asked Pat. 'I've not met him before.'

'That's Paul,' she said. 'He has a girlfriend,' she added, as if reading my mind.

'OK,' I said. 'He's cute, though. What does he do?'

'He runs an animation company in the West End. Pretty successful, actually. I've known him for years.'

Cute and tall and thin and arty and rich. And taken. Damn.

Jack interrupted my reverie. 'Ready for another dance?' he asked, grabbing my hand without waiting for an answer. As I walked towards the dance floor, I mentally filed Paul under 'Save for Later'.

I must have misfiled him under 'Forget Him', because that's just what I did, for two years. Then one day Pat tossed his name into a sentence.

'Paul came by today. I thought he wanted to see me, but instead he kept looking at your fucking book the whole time.' Pat told me he spotted *The Butcher, The Baker, The Candlestick Maker* on her coffee table, and asked to borrow it.

'Begged to borrow it, actually,' she said. 'I told him to buy his own. Hope you don't mind. Boost the sales and all.'

'Paul,' I said, momentarily diverted from the aphrodisiac of commerce. 'The cute guy from your Brazilian birthday party.'

'That's the one,' she said. 'He was asking about you, too. Wanted to know if you were single.'

'I thought he had a girlfriend.'

'Not any more,' she said. 'They broke up about a year ago.' She let that fact sink in, then told me he'd also asked for my number.

'I hope you gave it to him,' I said. 'He's gorgeous.'

'I thought I should ask you first. Guess *that* was unnecessary.'

'No, that's fine. Thanks, darling. Appreciate it,' I said.

I waited a nanosecond, so as not to sound too eager. 'You don't happen to have his number, do you?'

She did, and an hour later Paul and I had a date for later that evening. I invited him to join me for a night out with some pals. One of my girlfriends, Lucy, a singer/songwriter, was showcasing her music at Pop, a club in Soho, and had invited some friends along for support.

Paul walked into the club wearing a blue pinstriped suit over a white cotton T-shirt and a grey-and-blue tweed flat cap. He smiled when he saw me, and kissed me on both cheeks as he joined the table.

I didn't usually subject a first date to a night out with my mates, but I knew Paul would fit in. Based on that first night I met him, I knew he was easy going and smiley and clearly wasn't someone who couldn't handle strangers.

Except for the change of wardrobe, he looked no different from when I'd seen him two years earlier.

'Hi, stranger,' I said, looking into his big blue eyes. 'Good to see you again.' I knew he knew I meant it.

When the show ended at ten, the last place I wanted to go was home, at least alone. I proposed a visit to my home away from home. 'Shall we go to Soho House and get a bite to eat?' I said. 'I'm starving.'

Too late, I realised the wording of my request didn't leave

much room for a 'no', but in any case Paul seemed happy to stay by my side. So we drove to the House, took a seat at the Circle Bar, and ordered some chips and a couple of Pinot Grigios.

'I saw your book at Pat's,' he said, as we manoeuvred in to a couple of seats. 'Congratulations.'

'Thanks. I'm really pleased I wrote it,' I said. 'Although now I have to live with the repercussions. A lot of guys are afraid that if they talk to me, they'll end up in my second book. You're a brave man.'

'Now I have to read it,' he said. 'Do you have a copy you could lend me?'

'Probably, somewhere. Who knows?' I said, wondering if he wanted a loaner as an excuse to see me again, or if he was my second-worst nightmare, after tiny cocks: tight. 'It's only four pounds on Amazon, Paul. Go on, splurge!'

'But I'd rather have one signed by you, Suzanne. You're sort of famous now.'

There was something in Paul's tone that made me question his motives. Did he want me? Did he want to be with me because I was the author of an erotic memoir? I decided not to ponder and just go with the moment. I had wanted to meet this guy for two years, and now here he was, sipping a glass of wine across from me, ever so handsomely. If he was with me only so he could brag to his mates about having a drink with some chick who wrote about all the guys she'd fucked, so be it.

We ate our chips and sipped our wine until I noticed it was well past midnight. As it was a school night, I had already bypassed my mental curfew by a couple of hours.

'I really have to go,' I said. 'Maybe we can meet up on the weekend if you're around?'

'That sounds great,' he said. 'Can I walk you to your car?'

What a gent: attractive and gentlemanly.

My car was parked down a cul-de-sac off of Rathbone Place, itself a small road off Oxford Street. The street was deserted aside from my lone car.

As we reached the car Paul turned to kiss me, but instead of reaching for my lips, as I'd expected, he kissed my neck, leaving tiny butterfly kisses that barely touched my skin but tingled where his lips had made contact. He had one hand around my waist, pulling me towards him, whilst the other rested against the back of my head. His lips brushed across my neck from side to side. I had never been kissed like that before, and the effect was intoxicating. I tried to anticipate his next move, tilting my head, easing the collar of my sheepskin coat onto my shoulders, presenting the full length of my neck to him. I enjoyed the tenderness. It was lovely and intimate and unexpected. I didn't want him to stop.

'Turn around,' he said at last.

I obeyed and stood facing my car. I heard traffic in the distance, but the lights of the surrounding buildings were off, and a dim glow from a street lamp fifty yards away reminded us that we were not the only people in this world. I should be going, I thought, I have to get up early.

But I didn't want to leave Paul. I lay my head on the car's roof and dropped my shoulders to ease the coat off my back. It fell to the ground, a calculated theatrical gesture and no less sexy for it, I knew.

'You are terrible,' he said, laughing.

I felt his hands lift my hair, his lips touch the back of my neck, the warmth of his breath. His lips and tongue skated across the skin. I felt vulnerable and exposed, my neck suddenly feeling like the most intimate part of my body, Paul pressed into my back and moved his mouth across the nape of my neck.

The sound of distant footsteps interrupted Paul's kisses. I felt him pull away from me. The footsteps grew fainter almost as soon as we noticed them, and Paul returned to my neck.

'You have a beautiful neck,' he whispered into my skin. 'I'm shaking all over.'

I moaned in reply.

'Why didn't we get together two years ago?' he said.

'Probably because you had a girlfriend and I had a boyfriend,' I said, turning around. 'Just a theory.'

He smiled. Then we kissed. Paul's tongue darted around my mouth and brushed against my teeth and tongue. His kisses were soft and wet and made my head spin. This didn't feel like the beginning of a one-night stand. It felt special. I felt special. I'd waited two years to meet this spectacular man, and suddenly we were both available and interested. Finding a boyfriend was not a priority at that point in my life; after all, I was still seeing Greg and Brendan and Carl and Sam on a rotating basis. I didn't think I wanted a boyfriend, but I knew I wanted Paul. I was glad this was not a one-night stand. I had to see him again.

I said goodbye and got in the car. I drove away, watching Paul in my rear-view mirror.

The next day Paul rang my office. 'About that book,' he said. 'Can I come by and pick it up?'

'I'm not sure I want you to read it,' I said. 'I'm not sure it's a good idea that you know so much about me.'

At Soho House the night before, Paul had called himself a 'one-woman man'. He'd never cheated, he said, never had group sex, never done anything he thought was kinky. He said he liked the feeling of intimacy. He was 48 and had been having sex since he was 14. In those thirty-plus years, he had slept with fewer than ten women. His relationships tended to last for years, the very opposite of my one-night stands. In my head, I calculated that he'd had in his entire life as many partners as I went through in a month. We were complete opposites.

'No, I really want to read it,' he said. 'I know I can go out and buy it, but I'd rather get one from you.'

An hour later, he bicycled to my office and I handed over my last copy.

'I really appreciate you giving me this,' he said. 'You got the kids this weekend?'

'Yes,' I said. I looked at him, held his gaze. 'But I'm all yours next weekend.'

Three days later, we met at the Prince Albert, a pub near his flat in Hackney.

'Wow,' he said. 'The book. It was amazing.'

I felt embarrassed.

'I mean it, really,' he said. 'I don't know how you could go with some of those guys, though. Some of them were bloody assholes.'

I tried to explain that, at the time, I didn't really see them that way, didn't conduct personality tests in advance. 'I was horny,' I said. 'They were there.'

'I couldn't do that,' he said. 'But those guys, a lot of them ... they weren't even boyfriends.'

'Let's have a drink, Paul,' I said. I got the sense Paul didn't quite get me, which was surprising since he'd just read 240 pages about my life. I didn't have sex with men because I hoped they would become boyfriends. I had sex with men because that was what I enjoyed.

We had a few more rounds, and then it was closing time.

'Would you like to come back to mine?' Paul asked. 'I have some vodka and a joint.'

We walked the few streets over to his flat, then sat side by side on a long wooden bench that was pushed up against an eight-foot wooden table that looked like something out of an old school canteen. The décor was minimalist but comfy, with black-and-white photos on the walls, a big oil painting over a cream-coloured sofa and a long table that served as the centrepiece of the room. Paul lived in a converted synagogue, and his flat featured high ceilings and a large open-plan living space, with the bath and bedroom off of it. It was cool and comfortable. We smoked the joint and started kissing. Just like the first time we'd kissed by the car, I began to feel light-headed. After a few minutes, I actually thought I might faint. I laughed at the thought and pulled away from him.

'I think I'm going to have to lie down,' I said. 'I'm not joking. I really think I'm going to faint.'

'I'll come in with you,' he said, amused. Paul walked me to his bedroom.

He sat beside me and unbuttoned my jumper, starting at the neckline and moving down one button at a time. The buttons were small and he had difficulty pushing each one through its tiny hole. I had never unbuttoned the jumper myself, always slipping it over my head, but I enjoyed watching Paul's long slender fingers at work.

'Here,' I said, as he struggled with the final button, 'I'll help you.' I pulled my arms out of the sleeves and flung the jumper onto the floor next to the bed.

Paul moved towards my moulded black-lace bra next. He put his hands around me, then relaxed his embrace to caress my back. Then, in one quick gesture, he skilfully unclasped the three hooks and let the bra straps slide off my shoulders. I thought I heard him gasp as my bra hit the floor, revealing my breasts. He cupped one breast in his hand and gently kissed the nipple, letting his tongue linger for a while before moving onto the other one.

'You have lovely breasts, sweetheart,' he said, softly. I adored his deep voice and the faint Scottish accent that coloured his words. There was something about its pitch and tone I found a complete turn-on. The sound of his voice just drew me in. He used the word 'sweetheart' liberally, and although I know women who cringe at the word and some who find it patronising, I found it charming. Being with a man who had had only ten sex partners his entire life made me feel girlish, like I still had lots of growing up to do. He knew how to work a bra strap, but he still had an air of innocence about him.

Paul moved his hands down my waist and tried to unfasten a tacky belt I was wearing as a joke. It was gold and had a heart-shaped buckle studded with red, white and blue crystals set in the pattern of the American flag.

'I think you're going to have to help me here,' he said, so I did. I unclasped the belt, leaving Paul free to remove my jeans. Soon they joined the other clothing on the floor.

Paul paused to kiss me before sliding his hands down my glittery red knickers, a silly holiday treat I'd bought a few months ago and thought, as I'd dressed for our date, might amuse him.

'I'm wearing my Christmas pants,' I said.

He laughed. 'Very nice they are, too,' he said, before removing them for me.

Sitting on the side of the bed, I pulled Paul's T-shirt above his head, or tried to. He was much taller than I, so my arms weren't long enough to get the shirt over his head. But his jeans were easier, as they were loose and needed little assistance to slip off his body.

'I've lost tons of weight,' he said, apologising. 'I hope you like skinny men.

'I *love* skinny men,' I replied, truthfully, and slipped between the sheets.

I looked down at his briefs. His hard-on was clearly visible and I went to stroke the outside of the fabric. I was desperate to touch him, but Paul wouldn't let me.

'Wait,' he said. 'We have plenty of time.' He looked seriously at me. 'I want to *make love* to you.'

'Make love'. It must have been five years since I'd heard those two words used together. Most men just wanted to fuck me.

Paul pulled off his pants and climbed in next to me.

He crawled between my legs, and caressed my pussy with his tongue. It may have been the combination of the grass and alcohol, or it may have been because, for the first time in a very long time, I had met someone with whom I wanted to spend more than one night. Whatever it was, Paul's desire was contagious and I became lost in feeling his tongue around my clit.

'You're very good at that,' I whispered in between moans.

'I'm sure you've had better,' he said.

'No,' I said, truthfully. 'I really don't know that I have.'

He stayed between my legs for twenty minutes or more, then

grabbed a condom, rolled it over his cock, and slid himself into me. He was not big, not anywhere near what I was used to, but the pheromones dancing in my body more than made up for his size. I felt completely in tune with his body and his rhythm, letting him slide in and out of me while enjoying feeling him inside and hearing his breath quicken. The tension and pace increased with every stroke.

'I think you're amazing,' he said.

'Thanks, but I'm really not so special,' I said. 'I'm just Suzanne.'

'No, you're amazing, Suzanne.'

After about ten minutes Paul let out a tremendous scream. I had never heard anyone scream so loudly during sex before. I was amused. I took it as a compliment.

I didn't come but that was not unusual when I was with someone I liked a lot. I could orgasm quickly with swinging partners or strangers, but when my head and pheromones got involved, I become overstimulated, overexcited. I can't relax enough to come.

'That was some noise,' I said.

'I haven't come in ages,' he said. 'I don't wank.'

'What do you mean, you don't wank?' I'd never heard of a man who didn't. 'Why not?'

'It's not very comfortable,' he said. Paul explained that he had a medical problem that made masturbating uncomfortable. 'I've got an attached foreskin, and it's too tight around the head, so if there's too much pressure, sometimes it rips. It's really painful, so why bother?'

'Why don't you just get it sorted out?' I asked.

'You're right, I should,' he said, but then admitted he was nervous about it. 'What if something goes wrong? You know, it's … Down there.'

'It can't be that uncommon. Surely it's better to get it sorted out than to not be able to enjoy sex.'

'Don't worry about me, sweetheart. I just want to make you come.'

I told him I'd had too much to drink and that it wasn't going to happen.

I slept over that night and the next morning Paul woke up early to make me a cup of tea. He brought me some home-made oatmeal, stirred with raisins, seeds, and honey. It was delicious, in part because it was such a rare gesture. I couldn't remember the last time a man made me breakfast.

I smiled as I got back into my car. Cock problems aside, I felt like I'd met someone special.

14. NOT RIGHT

'He's not right for you, Suzanne,' Pat said. We were talking about my latest crush, Paul. He and I had been seeing each other for a couple of weeks, and I was giving her the latest.

'Why do you say that?' I said. 'He's your mate.'

'He's just not ... right,' she said. 'For you, I mean. You're too experienced for him, too dynamic. You wrote a book about your fucking life, for God's sake. Paul would never do that. He's actually rather boring.'

This was surprising news coming from the woman who'd given me her old buddy's number.

'Well, *I* don't think he's boring,' I said. 'I think he's great. I really like him. And he's a great kisser.'

Pat and Paul had known each other for a decade, since

working together on a film. Paul had given her a start in the industry at a time when she didn't know anyone. She'd just come to London from Ireland and was looking for work, and Paul was a big-cheese animator, running his own studio in Soho. He gave her some freelance assignments, and the friendship blossomed from there. Ironically, now she was animating her own pop videos, and his company had gone down and he was working part-time in retail, to boost his income.

'He doesn't even own a computer, Suzanne,' said Pat, piling on the evidence. 'He chucked it when he lost the company.'

'So?' I said. 'It's not his electronics I'm interested in.'

'How can you go out with a man that doesn't own a computer, especially someone who used to work in computer graphics? He can't receive emails, he can't go on the web – it's nuts. What kind of a person doesn't own a computer in the twenty-first fucking century?' she added. 'And he drinks too much.'

'Who doesn't? This is boozy Britannia. Aside from you, everyone drinks.'

Pat told me that the last time she'd seen Paul, he'd come over for a cup of tea and ended up drinking a fifth of whisky.

'It was the only booze I had in, since ... you know, the good ol' days. It was there for historic reasons.'

Pat had teetotalled for a decade. And after Paul poured her last sentimental bottle down his throat a couple of weeks earlier, she'd decided she didn't want to see him any more. Still, I questioned her motives. I wondered whether her advice to steer clear was impartial or based on a deeper desire to rid him completely from her life. She knew she'd never get Paul out of her life if he became a part of mine.

In any case, I've never been the type to take advice from friends. I prefer to make my own mistakes.

After Pat gave me his number, Paul and I spoke on the phone almost every day, and we got together for a bonk every kids-free weekend. But it always seemed to be me who took the initiative. I made the calls, and half the time Paul didn't pick up. When he did, I realised, I was the one doing most of the talking. It was a real reversal of the Suzanne–Max dynamic.

'I just like listening to you,' he said when I asked him why he was always so quiet. I could never quite shake the image I'd formed back on our first date in Soho House. He'd sat next to me wide-eyed and overly excited as I talked, at his prodding, about my life and book. He seemed almost star-struck, and that made me uneasy. I was hardly Jacqueline Susann.

And yet he introduced me to his friends as if I were. 'Suzanne is the most amazing woman I've ever met,' he said when we ran into his mates at his local. He did it on our first date, and on our second. By our third, I went from flattered to embarrassed. I began to suspect I wasn't a date, but a trophy. He told his buddies about my book. 'She wrote a best-selling book about her sex life and she has a blog that's read by thousands. She's the most famous person I've ever known.'

'Can we talk about something else, Paul? That's a large Chardonnay for me.'

Paul couldn't talk about me without mentioning my book or my blog, or promising to actually buy the book he obsessed over so publicly. But buying the book was always a future-tense event. He always asked to buy a dozen copies from me, at a discount, so he could give one to his friends.

'You'll get them cheaper on Amazon,' I said, half joking.

For someone who had seemed so keen on me, Paul, when it came to the phone, was like so many men I'd met before. He had a challenging relationship with his mobile. One of the guys I fucked regularly, a dancer named Pauli, who was a pal of Rump Shaker's, was capable only of responding to text messages. Brendan, a theatre director, took a minimum of three days to respond to his voice messages. John, the taxi driver, took six hours to respond to his, and then, like Pauli, got back only by text. The thought had crossed my mind to start an

Excel sheet just to keep track of the communications preferences of the men in my life. Some preferred voice, some preferred text, some just liked turning up when they were horny. Paul, I learned, just hated phones. But then, communication wasn't his forte.

After a few weeks and a few bonks, when I thought we'd become a regular thing, I called Paul for a catch-up. When a full day elapsed without hearing from him, I became concerned.

'Are you OK?' I asked when he finally rang back.

'What do you mean?'

'I left a couple of messages and, when I didn't hear from you, I thought maybe you'd fallen off your bike or that something dreadful had happened.'

'Oh sorry, sweetheart,' he said. 'I'm crap at communicating. I really am. But, actually, I'm surprised you care.'

'What do you mean, surprised I care?' I didn't want to say I'd thought we were dating, but the truth was, I had rather thought we were.

'Well, I've read your book. I didn't think you did the attached thing. I'm flattered.'

I didn't understand why he'd be flattered. I just thought he'd be happy that I cared. I realised that he defined me by my book and by my web blog, which he told me he read daily, and not by who I was. I was an author, or a character, but not a woman.

'Anyway,' said Paul, diverting. He told me that he'd left his phone at the bottom of his bag, on silent, and then forgotten about it. For a man who supposedly was looking for a better job, he didn't seem so anxious to check his messages. No email, phone switched off, I wondered if he expected prospective clients to get in touch with him by carrier pigeon. I was relieved that he was OK, but his laissez-faire attitude jarred with my own sensibilities. I've always believed that, if you're in a relationship with someone, a daily call is the least one should expect. Fuck buddies are different. I only hear from them, or they from me, when either of us wants sex. It caused pause that I heard from my fuck buddies more often than I heard from Paul.

'So, what are you up to Friday. You wanna get together? I'm meeting up with some friends at the pub.'

Pat's evidence of his unsuitability was beginning to stack up. Paul didn't like the phone, he didn't own a computer and, I soon found out, he didn't seem to want sex as much as he liked a drink.

Every time we got together and had sex, there were three of us in bed: Paul, me, and a bottle. We'd meet at the pub, stay until closing, and then wobble back to his flat for some after-hours action. I loved the way he kissed me, I loved his tenderness and the chemistry between us, but after the third time we 'made love' – to use his words – I wondered how much of the love was alcohol-induced and how much was real passion.

Then there was the issue of the orgasm. I rarely come when I'm drunk. But being with Paul meant being drunk. Thinking back on what Pat had said, I began to think that perhaps she was right.

'Do you realise we only fuck when we're pissed?' I said one morning. It was well after noon, after yet another night on the tiles, and yet another orgasm-free evening.

'No, we don't,' he said.

'Yes, we do,' I said. 'Think about it. We always meet at the pub. Always. And then we go back to yours. Drunk.'

Paul remained silent.

I've never needed to get drunk in order to get laid. Many of my friends do; they use alcohol or drugs as foreplay, and find my relative sobriety a hard thing to contemplate. To me, having a couple of drinks is great for releasing inhibitions and getting the party started, but, unlike many women, I've never found it necessary to drink away sex guilt. I don't have guilt; I know what I want, and alcohol is not going to make me want something any more than I already do. I can suck off a room full of men I've never met, in a sex club full of people I've never seen, and do it sober. I like cock a hell of a lot more than I like alcohol. I like the way a man's tongue feels on my clit, the endorphin high when a cock enters me or when I take one in my mouth. Alcohol dulls the sensations. It is the amateurs who need the boost; the men in my phone book, and the women and men I know from the swinging scene, are teetotallers. Sex is their high.

Paul didn't return my calls on schedule. He drank too much. And, to round it off, there was the penis problem. Despite his coming, loudly, the first night we were together, the encounters that followed were marred by the foreskin issue. Paul would enter me and then, without warning, usually about five minutes into it and always in the mish, suddenly pull out and scream in agony.

'Sorry, sweetheart,' he'd say, when he could finally speak. 'It really hurts.'

'That's OK,' I'd say, in my concerned Florence Nightingale voice. I knew that was the end of the evening's entertainment.

Paul would roll off of me and we'd have a cuddle.

I'd never found myself so frustrated as when Paul and I were in bed together. We'd be fucking but, instead of relaxing into the sensations, I'd be worrying that he wasn't getting any pleasure out of it. And I'd find myself waiting for the moment when he'd scream.

At some point, just a few minutes into a fuck but long before my orgasm would kick in, I'd be thinking about the skin around the head of his cock and how it might tear from too much friction. I couldn't relax and he didn't really want to come.

Two months after our first date, I realised the situation was grim. Yet, in an attempt to salvage the relationship, I invited Paul to join me and my kids in India for the Christmas holidays. London wasn't working for us, but I hoped a spell on the beach would be the Band-Aid our relationship needed.

'How much is that going to cost?' he said.

'About seventeen hundred pounds,' I said. 'But it's a five-star hotel, and it's on the south coast. It's gorgeous.'

'God,' he said. He waited a full thirty seconds before continuing. 'I couldn't spend that much on a holiday. I've *never* spent that much on a holiday. That's just not me. Sorry, sweetheart.'

So much for the geographical cure. 'OK, understood,' I said. 'I'll send you a postcard.'

All signs pointed to the exit, and to my portfolio of men collecting dust in the background of my mind. I had to admit what I already knew: I needed a man who could enjoy sex, a man who could make me come. I could be a one-man woman for the right guy. Unfortunately, Paul wasn't that guy.

I'd jumped off the merry-go-round of men but, instead of finding respite, I got the itch that made me want to jump back on again.

I hadn't had a monogamous relationship since Karume. I had tried to fit into my Mr Contender box a man who didn't belong there. Waiting for the phone to ring, having sex in the missionary position, getting drunk as a precursor to having sex, then dreading the shriek that brought it all to an end – none of that was for me. If the sex had been mind-blowing or kinky, or even merely satisfying, I might have given it a chance. The truth was, I'd found Paul attractive and sexy and cool, but once the loved-up phase had worn off, I had to admit we were just too different.

After all, on top of the other issues, Paul was not the type to understand my having other lovers.

'I've never dated more than one girl at a time,' he once told me, after admitting he couldn't comprehend my having a portfolio of guys. He knew, having read my book, that I wasn't big on monogamy.

I explained that I could be monogamous, and had been during periods in my life, but this was probably not destined to be one of them. After a while I realized it wasn't what I wanted. I could not see myself in a conventional relationship, not now, not yet.

I don't think Paul could even comprehend that concept. It was too far removed from his own experience. He found it exciting to be with someone whose life had been so different from his own, but unlike some of my regular playmates, he didn't want to be a part of that journey, and wasn't quite able to understand it. I came to the conclusion he enjoyed reading about himself in my blog more than being with me. I suspected it made him feel like a minor celeb in my very small world.

I missed my kinky playpals: Carl, who loved it when I sucked him off in a steam room in front of an audience; Sam, who blindfolded me and fucked me in the ass; and Greg, who always talked dirty at just the right moment. They made me laugh. They made me come. I didn't have to think about whether they would ring or like my kids or come on holiday with me. I'd compromised who I was during my ten-year marriage and with the live-ins who followed, and I'd gotten burned in the process. Now, older and wiser, I wasn't about to settle any more. I'd been having a fine time before Paul came along.

More importantly, I preferred being single. There was no brain damage attached to it. With Paul, it was all about expectation. Will he call me back? Was he going to be around over my kids-free weekend? Was I ever going to have orgasm?

Pat was right, of course. Sensible Pat. Paul wasn't the one for me.

I stopped calling him for our biweekly dates. And, as usual, he did not call. But now and then I found myself thirsty and in the mood for a booze-up. I may have lost a lover, but at least I gained a reliable drinking buddy.

15. PAIN SLUT

'Do you like older men?'

I was sitting in the Angel Inn, a gastro pub in Highgate, having a post-work drink at the request of someone who'd read and liked my book. I was used to male readers asking to meet me, and equally used to declining their invitations. Most of the guys seemed interested, not in me, but in auditioning for a role in my next book.

Tonight's drinking partner was a double novelty – a fan who wasn't interested in a star fuck and a fan who wasn't a man.

I'd been checking out a handsome executive leaning against the bar, one of many young suits on view that I half-hoped would catch my eye. So Emma's use of the word 'older' clashed with the visuals.

Emma and I met through a mutual friend, Emily. The two

women were journalists and, like most journalists I knew, they were savvy, witty and opinionated, as able to talk about sex and culture as about the court diary and current events. They met at a media bash and after a few glasses of wine discovered they'd both read my book. When Emily mentioned she knew me, Emma asked her to put us in touch.

'I LOVED your book,' she wrote. I loved her capitalisation. 'I found it unputdownable.' I found her vocabulary appealing. 'I would really love to meet you to compare notes and literary experiences.' I wanted to meet a fellow writer who not only liked my work but who didn't want to fuck me.

Half an hour after meeting at the pub, Emma and I were talking like old friends. Quickly, we discovered we were both Jewish girls, both 'cockists' – as Emma liked to describe girls who liked big cocks – and both had our share of dating disasters. There's nothing like swapping cock tales over cocktails to bond two women. We'd begun the night talking a bit about my book, then slipped into a chinwag about our jobs, but after a couple more drinks, the girltalk quickly turned to boytalk.

'Do I like older men?' I said. I thought of Max. 'Well, I went out with a youngish fifty-four once, and that was OK.'

Emma smiled.

'How about you?' I said pondering Emma's question. 'How old is "old"?'

'Sixty,' she said, adding quickly, 'a very *young* sixty.'

I had been expecting a generic riff on the wonders and horrors of going out with geriatrics, but it was clear Emma wasn't talking generics. She had a specific man in mind.

'I suppose I could stretch to sixty.' I laughed. 'What's he like?'

'Well,' she said, leaning forwards on her elbows and launching into sales mode. 'He's handsome, quite well known, very nice. He's a gynaecologist, so he knows a few things about women.'

'Funny?' I said, intrigued and hopeful.

'Um,' she said. 'I suppose he can be.'

'In other words, he's not funny,' I said, hopes dashed. 'Not a laugh a minute, not quick witted.'

'Well, no,' she admitted. 'He's not hysterically funny. But he's interesting. I think you'll like him.'

'Have *you* fucked him?' I asked. 'Does he have a big cock?'

'No,' she said.

'Which one is it? No, you haven't fucked him, or no, he doesn't have a big cock?'

'No and I don't know.' Emma laughed. 'We almost got there, but it didn't happen. We just had a bit of a snog.' Emma paused a second and arched her eyebrows. 'He *says* he has a big cock. But he's a bit too kinky for me.'

'Kinky?' I said, suddenly interested. I hadn't heard that word in a while, not since before Paul anyway. 'How kinky?'

'Well, that's for you to find out,' she said and laughed.

'I don't like peeing on people. I can't do that.'

'I'm sure if you tell him you won't pee on him, he'll be OK with that,' she said. Suddenly serious, she added, 'So, can I give him your email address?'

'Go ahead,' I said. 'Why not?'

'Great!' said Emma, genuinely excited. Her inner Yenta had surfaced and scored a hit. 'I think you're really going to hit it off. Will you let me know what happens?'

'Of course!'

The next day I found an email from Christopher in my inbox.

'Dear Suzanne,' I read. 'My adored friend Emma says you wouldn't mind horribly if I invited you out for a drink/coffee/tea/dinner sometime soon. I hope this is not one of her practical jokes, because you sound so delightful. I am around for the next few days if you think our paths might cross.'

I Googled Christopher's name and checked out the photos that popped up onscreen. Distinguished bald top, boulders for cheekbones, saucer eyes. I could do older, I decided.

'Dear Christopher,' I wrote back. 'No, it's not a practical

joke. I really am delightful. ☺ And this is my kids-free weekend. What about Sunday lunch?'

We arranged to meet at the Wells Tavern in Hampstead, one of the many recently refurbished gastropubs in the heart of Hampstead village. Christopher had booked a table in the posh upstairs dining room, I discovered on arrival, and I was delighted at what promised to be a rare treat. I was slightly taken aback when brought to the table, as the man who introduced himself to me looked at least a decade older than any of the photos I'd found on the web. He was about six-feet tall, medium built, with bright blue eyes. He was not unattractive, but I'd never been out with anyone in his sixties before and suddenly found myself thinking I might not be ready to, either.

I sat down as Christopher ordered a bottle of burgundy from the waiter. Then he pulled out a dog-eared copy of my book.

'I see you came prepared, sir.'

'Yes, and it was an interesting read,' said Christopher. 'I've made a few notes.' As he opened the book I noticed pages where he'd highlighted sentences. I'd expected a casual lunch, but suddenly it was beginning to feel like work.

Is this guy going to interview me? I wondered. Something in my expression must have tipped him off, because as soon as he'd picked up the book, he'd put it back down.

'We can talk about this later,' he said. 'Let's order, shall we?'

I ordered the Sunday special – roast beef and Yorkshire pudding – then settled into the leather chair. I was wearing a clingy chocolate-brown dress and matching heels. The dress was low cut, but I noticed, halfway through the roast, whilst glancing down at my plate, that it revealed a little more cleavage than I'd wanted Christopher – or the rest of the diners – to see. And see he did.

'You have lovely breasts,' said Christopher, leaning over the table to whisper close to my face. His voice was intoxicating, a classic BBC radio voice – smooth and deep and confident and lush. I hadn't even noticed its allure until the comment on my breasts. Suddenly Christopher went from an old man to a sexual man. He became as different to the eye as to the ear.

'Thank you,' I said and smiled, staring into his pale-blue eyes whilst thinking that perhaps sixty wasn't *so* old after all.

His was a voice I could have listened to for hours, and that afternoon, I did. Four hours after my arrival, suddenly aware ours were the only voices, we looked around and saw there was no one else in the dining room.

'Shall we go back to mine for a coffee?' Christopher asked.

'Lead the way,' I said, standing up, smiling, and taking his arm.

Christopher lived in a cosy two-bedroom flat at the back of a large mansion block that looked out onto Hampstead Heath. It was furnished just as one would expect of a man Christopher's age – a mixture of antiques and flowery upholstery, with vintage horticulture prints on the wall and worn Orientals on the floor. I walked towards the love seat in the front room.

'Why don't you take your shoes off,' he said as I eased into the two-seater.

I removed my lace-ups. Christopher sat at my feet and began massaging them.

'That feels lovely,' I said, leaning back into the sofa. I opened my legs to reveal my pussy to him. As usual, I'd foregone the underwear when dressing for our meeting. 'My feet were killing me. You're bringing everything back to life.'

'Every woman needs a man in her life who can rub her feet,' he said.

'I couldn't agree more. A man at my feet. I like that.'

One of Christopher's hands travelled up my leg, massaging my muscles as he did so. When he reached my pussy, I looked down just in time to see his bald head disappear up my dress.

I sat back and let him continue. I spread my legs further apart and felt his tongue rest against my clit. I knew from Emma that Christopher was an experienced lover. Her parting words were about Christopher. In his prime, she said, he had been a real player and had slept with hundreds of women. I soon learned she was probably right. After our initial email exchange, Christopher had sent me photos – almost as old as his furniture, I now thought, guiltily, bitchily – that dated from when he was in his twenties. In his prime, Christopher had been magnificent – long dark curly hair, a lean, toned body, model-handsome. Judging by the way he used his tongue on my clit, I knew he'd put in some time on the stud farm, too.

'Oh, Christopher, that feels so good,' I said. 'You've obviously done this before.' I laughed in between moans.

'Just a few times. Why don't we go into the bedroom?' he said. 'It's more comfortable there. And we can take off our clothes.'

I got off the love seat and followed Christopher to the bedroom. It was dominated by a massive king-size bed with an antique brass bedstead. The sheets and pillows were forest green, very masculine. A built-in wardrobe ran down one side of the room and a narrow chest of drawers stood beside the bed.

I pulled off my clothes and Christopher pulled off his, revealing a tight hairless body and a medium-sized, medium-width, hard cock. Not a monster, not what I had expected, based on Emma's PR, but not tragic either.

I climbed on the bed, lay on my back and spread my legs. Christopher joined me and returned to position between my legs. He lapped at my clit and around my pussy, teasing me until I was dripping.

'Please,' I begged after fifteen minutes, after I'd felt my pussy expand and demand that it be filled by something or someone. 'Please put your fingers inside me.'

'Oh,' he said in a teasing tone. 'I think you should wait.'

'Pleeeease,' I begged.

'How much do you want it?'

'I want . . . I want it . . . I . . .'

'You're going to have to wait.' He continued rubbing his fingers on my clit.

'No,' I was moaning like a porn actress, except I wasn't acting. 'I don't think I can wait.' I loved that a sixty-year-old had me moaning. And I loved what he was doing.

Suddenly, Christopher stood up and opened a drawer next to his bed. I looked over and saw inside an impressive range of paraphernalia – nipple clamps and needles, dildos and butt plugs of various shapes and sizes. He opened another drawer and pulled out a dildo the size of my lower arm.

'What about this?' he said, smirking.

'For me or for you?' I said, half joking. I hoped he wasn't serious about using that gigantor on me. 'I couldn't take a thing that big.'

'Oh, I've taken this,' he said. 'It's actually very nice.'

Christopher's tone had turned smug; his expression straight faced. He had merely voiced a fact, and displayed his toy chest as if expecting me to be impressed. Which, I had to admit, I was. I'd never met a man who could take an entire rubber forearm up his ass.

'This is nice, too,' he said, and pulled out a torpedo-shaped butt plug that was two-thirds the length of a beer bottle and twice as thick.

Emma's words came back to me: 'He's a bit kinky.'

Oh, God, I thought. He's even kinkier than I am.

I wasn't particularly interested in the rubber arm or the military-issue bum blaster. 'What about your cock?' I said. 'That would do.'

'No,' said Christopher, firmly. 'You'll have to wait for that.' He reached over to his toy drawer and pulled an eight-inch dildo from his stash. I was grateful that he had found my preferred size.

Christopher climbed back onto the bed, grabbed a tube of KY from the side cabinet, and lubed the dildo. Then he gently, expertly, eased it into my pussy. Meanwhile, his tongue resumed working my clit. I lay back and enjoyed having a pussy-professional in bed with me. I was no longer thinking about Christopher's age. I was thinking about his cock and how nice it would feel inside me.

Yet Christopher seemed to be in no rush to fuck and, after another fifteen minutes licking my pussy, I was in no rush for him to fuck me either. If he was happy down there, so was I. He was a master at oral, and feeling his tongue between my legs, circling my clit and massaging my pussy, the dildo moving in and out of me, sent energy surging through my pussy. I could feel myself dripping all over the dildo as Christopher pushed it in and out, in and out, in and out.

'I really want to feel your *cock*,' I said at last. If something was going to be inside me, I preferred the sensation of something warm and human to the chill of rubber.

Christopher pulled the dildo out. 'You want this?' he said, sitting up on his knees, holding out his hard cock and aiming it in my direction.

'Yes.'

Christopher eased himself into me, first one inch, then one inch more.

'And this?' He eased in another inch.

I moaned. 'Yes. Please.'

He eased himself in more, then a bit more, until he was fully inside me. I moaned loudly as I felt the intense pleasure that comes from being filled by a man.

'You want to be my slut?' he said.

'Yes,' I moaned. I lay back and spread my legs in a V. 'Yes. I want to be your slut.'

'You'll have to do what I tell you to do, then,' he said. 'Think you can do that?'

I said I thought I could and, at that moment, I wanted to. Christopher was a challenge to me. I'd never played the submissive role so completely before, but I'd fantasised about it often enough. I was invariably the one in charge at work and at home, the one who had to tell others what to do. For a change, I wanted to relinquish that control. Christopher, I figured, might be the perfect master. He seemed to like playing the big top, and I liked the idea.

Christopher and I continued to connect every few days following that first afternoon together and, each time, we played out new kinky games. He knew I was chasing my kink and was happy to help put me on the path. Each meet pushed my boundaries a little farther, progressing from simple teasing to tantric to role-playing to pain.

One evening, while I was grinding on his dick, Christopher reached into his toy chest and pulled out a pair of adjustable nipple clamps. I knew what they were, having seen plenty of them at fetish fairs I'd attended in the past. I'd never tried them, though; they just didn't appeal to me. My nipples aren't that sensitive, but if a guy wants to squeeze them, I'd rather he did it the old-fashioned way, with his fingers.

'Those look interesting,' I said. At that moment, while the endorphins were kicking around, I thought, What the hell.

'Don't worry, Suzanne. This is the beginner model. I wouldn't dare put the ones I use on you.'

He put a clamp on each of my nipples and slowly tightened the screws. It hurt. After a few minutes my nipples went numb, because the blood had stopped flowing to the tips. Christopher tugged on the chain linking the two clamps. That really hurt. Then he carried on fucking me, occasionally pausing to gently tweak the chain. The idea was that the pain-pleasure sensors would get confused and send a surge of endorphins through my body. I never quite got there. It just hurt all the time, not so much that I screamed, not that I even wanted to scream, but the clamps hurt in a way I wasn't used to. I didn't find the experience particularly interesting, although grinding on his cock felt pretty good. But then, grinding on any man's cock feels pretty good to me.

Despite the pain, the clamps did have one surprising effect on me: every time Christopher yanked on the chain, my pussy tightened around his cock. So as a science experiment, it was interesting. But as a party trick to repeat, I wasn't so sure.

We were still fucking when Christopher once again reached into the drawer and pulled out two crocodile clips, tiny nipple clips with sharp teeth that dig into the skin and take nipple play to a level I didn't even want to think about. Just looking at them made me feel ill.

Christopher instructed me on how to apply the clamps to his nipples. I put a clamp on his right nipple and watched the teeth dig into the flesh. His face tensed up.

'That has got to really hurt,' I said. 'That has really got to hurt.'

'Only for a moment, darling,' he said. 'I've been doing this for a while, remember.'

I said nothing more. I just carried on grinding.

'I'm a bit of a pain slut, if you haven't noticed,' Christopher added.

I'll say, I thought.

I felt Christopher's cock get harder inside me as I applied the second clamp. I felt like a newbie, recoiling as I watched him take the pain. But Christopher seemed to really enjoy it, and I enjoyed learning something new, I guess. The lesson was that pain just wasn't my thing.

That evening I rode Christopher for three hours, grinding on his cock and playing with his nipples, holding back my orgasm. Sometimes when you don't have a big cock inside you, it can take a while. Eventually I came. Christopher had incredible stamina, never once going soft, even though most of the time I barely moved whilst on top of him. That position, or the lack of stimulus, tends to shrink the cocks of a lot of guys I've been with.

I came to look forward to our evenings together. Christopher lived close by, so it was easy to pop over for a quickie, or a three-hour longie, as was usually the case. But then my kids returned from spending a few weeks abroad with their father, and I went back to my bimonthly sex schedule. When the first of my kids-free weekends approached, I rang Christopher to see if he was free for another longie.

'Weekends are absolutely dreadful for me,' he said. 'I usually go down to the country to spend time with my family.'

Family? I didn't know what family he was referring to. Emma had implied Christopher was totally available. Now I got the feeling he had a secret life – secret from me, anyway.

'Oh,' I said.

'But I'm free during the week.'

'But I'm not. I've got two kids.' I explained that I only did the weekend-date thing.

'Well, I'm around in the evenings, Suzanne,' Christopher countered. 'We could see each other then.'

He clearly wasn't hearing what I was saying. 'Christopher,' I said, 'I have *homework* on weeknights. Just let me know when you'll be in town on a weekend.'

The following week Christopher called me at work. 'Want to meet me for lunch? I want to take you shopping.'

I thought Jimmy Choos. I thought sexy lingerie from Agent Provocateur. I didn't think a field trip to a BDSM supermarket.

'Meet me at ninety Holloway Road.'

The only interesting place I knew on the Holloway Road was House of Harlot, a high-end shop selling designer fetishwear. Instead, I found myself at the front door of Fettered Pleasures. It was a shop I must have passed a hundred times but never noticed. The building was nondescript. There were no window displays. In fact, the windows had grilles over them. I had to press a buzzer to get through the front door.

Christopher was already inside when I got buzzed in. He was standing by the front counter, next to the cock rings and poppers.

The place was a cornucopia of every possible piece of equipment a person could punish another person with. There were dozens of floggers, paddles, whips, and birches on one wall, running down the length of the store. Glass cabinets were filled with cock-and-ball torture devices, cock cages, massive dildos and catheters. I saw steel butt plugs and electro-stim devices. There were carousels of gimp masks. Full-rubber suits, corsets, leatherwear and adult-size baby clothes hung from racks in the middle of the room.

'This is what we need,' Christopher said.

I couldn't believe the range of products there, and now I wondered which merchandise he was referring to.

Christopher pointed to a rack of elbow-length rubber gloves that came in every colour of the rainbow.

'I like these lilac ones,' I said, secretly adding to myself, for the washing-up.

Then I noticed a small acrylic butt plug in one of the glass cases. That, I could handle. I felt it better to point Christopher in the direction of stuff I liked. If he was going to take me shopping, at least it should be for something I'd actually use. I've always liked sticking small objects in my ass, and I didn't own anything in acrylic. The only toys I had at home were silicon, and I rather fancied the hard clean lines of the acrylic models.

'It's settled then,' said Christopher. 'A butt plug for you, and some rubber gloves you can use on me. The lilac ones?'

'Great,' I said.

As we walked out the door, Christopher handed me the package. 'Here you go,' he said, smiling.

'No, you keep it. For the next time I see you.'

But by the time we'd left that shop, I'd already decided I wasn't going to see him again. I knew what the rubber gloves were for, and I realised I had no desire to stick my fist up his ass. Or anyone else's. Despite thinking of myself as the girl who would try anything at least once, I realised there are some places where I just don't want to go.

16. THE TOUR GUIDE

Holiday romances always seem to happen to other people, never to me. Or almost never.

When I was in my twenties, I met a beefy Italian on the Greek island of Skiathos. It was my first grown-up trip abroad, so it seemed natural that I'd meet a handsome guy with a foreign accent in an exotic faraway place and speak the international language of love – in bed. But he turned out to be a premature ejaculator. His cock would get hard, and just as he was ready to enter me, he'd come. It was a frustrating relationship that lasted only slightly longer than it took him to climax. So Julio didn't quite count as a holiday romance.

Neither did the guys I'd slept with on business trips to America. I often had great luck mixing business with pleasure, but on solo holidays, all I got were sunburns and hangovers and maxed-out credit cards. As far as I was concerned, when it came to holiday humps, my tally remained at nil.

That's why, after booking a week's holiday in Raleigh, North Carolina, I set up ten internet dates. I figured the odds were good that at least two would come through. I figured I had nothing to lose by putting an ad' out there.

Craigslist had come through for me before on business trips, but it wasn't always so easy. Typically, the guys I followed up with were married or busy or both. It's easy for a man to say 'It'll be great to see you,' when the woman he's writing to is three thousand miles away. But when the mileage, like a cock in cold water, shrinks, the truth comes out.

I knew my brother Harry and his wife didn't get out much. Lisa was working towards a psychology degree and studied every night. Harry liked to hang out with his stepson and watch the basketball on the television. I knew my sons, who would accompany me during their Easter holidays, would be happy to park on the sofa next to them, even if it wasn't Arsenal throwing the ball around. I had to come up with my own entertainment, and that was a real challenge in a town where the annual high was being invited to the Cheesecake Factory restaurant's anniversary party in the Crabtree Valley Mall.

I wanted a tour guide, a good ol' American boy who'd share his own personal highlights with me. I got on Craigslist and posted an ad under the 'Casual Encounters' w-4-m section: 'London media chick, 46, 34DD, blonde with blue eyes, visiting Raleigh for a week. Looking for a VWE, handsome guy, 38–50, to show me the town and have some fun.'

Within a day I had ten hopefuls. One guy invited me to a swingers' party, but the 'hey, baby' come-on was a cliché turn-off. I just wanted a normal date, with one person. Another guy asked if I was into bondage, which was a downer after my kinkathons with Christopher. One respondent was 28 years old – too young. Others, I decided after viewing their pictures, were either too fat or too bland. I began to suspect my holiday losing streak was destined to remain unbroken.

Then another 24 hours went by. Amidst the nos was one yes: a response from a 37 year old guy who described himself as a part-time fireman. He said he wanted to show me his eight-inch hose.

I wanted him to show it to me, too, and, after seeing the pic, I thought, You're on, sergeant.

He looked like a lumberjack – muscles, moustache, big grin, plaid shirt – right out of the 1970s commercials for Swanson's Hungry Man frozen dinners. Stuck in a time warp, perhaps, but attractive enough for one date. Plus, I knew I might never again get the opportunity to fuck an icon, the great American fireman.

His name was Tom. We arranged to have dinner together a few days after I arrived.

'As long as it's not the Cheesecake Factory,' I wrote. Tom promised he'd come up with something more creative.

'Do you mind watching the kids?' I asked my sister-in-law and brother. 'I have a date tonight.'

Lisa stared at me in disbelief. 'What do you mean, you have a date?'

'I arranged it in London, through the web,' I said. 'Cute guy, a fireman. He's taking me to some Italian restaurant, the West Italian Café.'

'Oh, very nice.' Lisa sounded almost jealous. 'It's one of the nicest places in Raleigh. Enjoy.'

'I better. In the past five years, I've been to ten different countries and scored a total of zero times,' I said. 'I think it's time for a change, don't you?

Lisa laughed. My brother rolled his eyes.

I dressed in my tried-and-tested dinner-date outfit, which I'd brought from London just for the occasion – a sleeveless Miss Sixty denim dress, deep V-neck, knee length, and tight, set off by high-heeled sandals. The dress accented my cleavage and curves, whilst the heels elongated my calves and drew attention to my slim ankles. It was an outfit designed to arouse a man's interest. I painted my toenails fire-truck red in Tom's honour.

I arrived at the restaurant early, having budgeted extra time in case I had trouble finding the place. I waited outside, quite aware that, standing on a street corner in fuck-me heels and a flashy dress, I looked like a hooker. Men passed by, flashing me a look that said, 'I'd pay for it.' Good, that meant I'd dressed right. I had learned since my divorce that if a woman wants to get laid, she should dress like a woman who gets paid.

Ten minutes after the target hour, a man pulled up in an SUV and poked his head out the window. 'Hi!' he said. It was Tom, smiling. He looked exactly like his picture. That made me happy. Too many guys turn up either looking so different than their pic that they're unrecognisable, or acting too keen, too smiley, or too shy – the troika of turn-offs.

Our table wasn't ready, so we went to the bar. The West Italian Café had been fitted out of an old warehouse – the exposed-brick, open-plan look I'd seen in restaurants from Hoxton to TriBeCa to Fisherman's Wharf. Not exactly original but chic enough, as were the people around us, I noticed. It was the after-work crowd of women in little black dresses and men in blue blazers. I clashed, but then so did Tom. He was wearing a check shirt and chinos.

'So, this is Raleigh' said Tom, picking up his wine glass. 'What would you like to do after we eat?'

We'd not even begun dinner and already he was thinking of dessert.

Fucking came to mind, but instead I played it conservative. 'Do you know any good jazz clubs?'

'Afraid not,' said Tom. 'I like jazz, honey, I really, really do. But I have never heard any live jazz 'round these parts. That's New Orleans. Y'all in Raleigh now.'

That was that. I felt a pang of disappointment. But I figured that if we had to skip the jazz, then maybe going straight to the pudding wouldn't be the worst thing.

'Maybe we should ask someone,' said Tom. He turned to the woman with big blonde hair in a big black dress sitting next to us. 'Excuse me, ma'am. Do you happen to know where we might hear some jazz?'

'Jazz,' she said. 'Hmm. Let me think.' She thought for a minute, then mentioned two places known for playing music, one of which, the Blue Martini, sounded familiar to Tom.

'The Blue Martini it is, then,' I said, excited that I would be hearing some live music after four days of North Carolina AOR.

We moved to the dining room. I picked through my seafood platter, and Tom tucked into his spaghetti carbonara. More wine arrived with dinner, and I was glad for the alcohol, as Tom wasn't a big talker when there was food in front of him. I knew a few glasses of wine would help us both.

Wow, I thought, this is like a proper date.

Aside from my four-hour lunch with Christopher, it was rare that any of my dates involved food. I'd learned, after placing a few ads on Swinging Heaven specifying 'adult fun and dinner', that although I might see some meat on those dates, I should not expect a meal.

But at least when I had an appetite I did something to sate it. The businessmen at the next table looked starved; they kept glancing over at me, or rather at my cleavage. Were breasts so rarely displayed in Raleigh? Tom was a gentleman. He tried not to look at my breasts too often.

'So, do you find dates on Craigslist often?' I asked. I knew it wasn't the greatest conversation prompt, but it was about the only thing I knew we had in common.

'No, not often,' he said. 'But I'm living with my sister at the moment, until I buy a place, so it's a bit difficult to take women home anyway. If you know what I mean.'

I knew what he meant. And I found it odd that a man in his

late thirties didn't have his own place. Odd, too, that a man who didn't have his own place would want to take an equally homeless visitor out for dinner.

'Too bad I'm staying at my brother's,' I said. 'That place is out of the question, too.'

Tom bit on his lip. I wondered how we'd get to the pudding.

After leaving the restaurant we drove straight to the Blue Martini, but we arrived just as the band was packing up for the night. It was only 9.30.

'Sorry, hon,' Tom said. 'Looks like we got ourselves here just in time to be too late.' He asked if there was anything else I wanted to do.

'What about a strip club?' I was half joking, but at least those places could be counted on to stay open late and keep the liquor flowing. 'I've never been to an American strip club before, but most of the American movies I've seen lately, and every episode of *The Sopranos*, seems to feature one. I'd feel deprived if I left without experiencing this bit of Americana.'

Tom tried not to look surprised by my request – or too knowledgeable.

'Well . . .' he began.

'Well?'

He hesitated before speaking. 'There's the Golden Rose.'

'OK.'

Silence for a moment. 'That's the mid-range place,' he continued. 'The Dollhouse is more downmarket. And then there's the Foxy Lady.'

'Which one is the closest?'

'Golden Rose.'

'Done.'

We jumped in the SUV and drove to the Golden Rose. I was excited. I was also nervous. I assumed there would be no girls there, aside from the working girls.

The Golden Rose was in a lonely one-storey building in the middle of a car park, set opposite a shopping mall and a furniture salesroom. All the spaces were taken, so Tom drove over to the furniture store and parked.

I stepped out of the car and into a puddle. 'Shit,' I muttered.

'What?'

'It's all muddy here. Great parking space, Tom.'

'Sorry, Suzanne, honey. I'll make it up to ya.'

I hobbled over to the club. We walked through the door and into a small reception area. A middle-aged Southern woman was sitting behind a window. She looked at me and my tits, then at Tom.

'Are you a member?' she asked him.

'No, ma'am.'

'Then it's twenty dollars for you. She gets in free,' she said, pushing a piece of paper towards Tom. 'Fill in this form.'

While he bought a 'temporary membership' that somehow satisfied North Carolina's no-sin laws, I checked out a poster on a wall announcing the special appearance that night by a Playboy Playmate named Tiffany or Angel or Kylie. I could hear whoops and hollers coming from inside the club. It sounded like an American Western, and a busy night.

Now an official member of the Golden Rose, Tom took my arm and escorted me into a cavernous room filled with small round tables and black-and-white cushioned chairs. It was very dark in there, as the main illumination came from the small spotlights that directed everyone's focus to the stage. From what I could see, which was not much, I was the only female punter there, although my eyes caught the sparkles on the outfits of about a dozen strippers scattered about the room. They were in various stages of undress, wandering to and fro, sitting on customers' laps or giving 'private dances' in the rear. The men in the room were as young as 25 and no older than 50, many of them wearing baseball caps. No suits. These guys all looked as if they'd have been home cracking a Bud and watching the Sports Network had they not dropped in for a peek at Tiffany/Angel/Kylie.

I giggled nervously.

Tom and I sat at a table in the back. Immediately a very cute, very slim waitress wobbled over in super-high fuck-me heels to take our order. She was wearing an incredibly short red skirt and a matching crop top, and had to scream to be heard above Missy Elliott's 'Get Ur Freak On'.

'What?' she said. 'Excuse me?'

No wonder the focus was on the stage. Who could talk? Guess I wasn't going to hear Tom's autobiography.

I was grinning like the Cheshire Cat. I just couldn't stop smiling, partly thanks to nerves and feeling so outnumbered and partly because I found the whole environment so amusing. It was something of a cliché, just like it's depicted in the movies and on TV, just as I'd imagined it would be – the off-duty blue-collar workers, slouching in their chairs, drinking beer, watching the girls, whooping it up.

I like looking at beautiful girls, especially girls who have curves, big breasts and long slim legs and who want to be watched. I'd tried the girl-on-girl action during college and, though it doesn't really turn me on any more, I still get vicarious thrills from looking at sexy women. And so did Tom. He was happy to look at the display models, cute or not, and perhaps just as happy not to have to talk. The music pounded, the girls wiggled, Tom and I laughed.

I was happy about the way the night was turning out. A visit to a strip club ranked high on my list of tourist experiences. As for Tom, it must have been his lucky day, too. I doubted many girls asked the local boys to take them to a place full of gorgeous girls, at least not on the first date.

We watched dancers writhe in mock ecstasy as they made love to the poles fixed to the stage. Some looked like they might actually be enjoying their job, but on the whole I sensed an utter lack of interest, as if, given the choice and the same amount of money, the girls would just as soon work behind the till at Sainsbury's.

About twenty minutes after we ordered them, our drinks arrived: a bloody Mary for me, a Budweiser for Tom. We'd so enjoyed the action, we hadn't even noticed our drinks hadn't come.

The girls were a real mixed bag. Some were very thin and looked like they'd surpassed mere anorexia and bottomed out with a bad drug habit. Others had big hips and round bottoms and looked like Amazons in comparison. A tiny black girl in a microscopic bikini walked around the room serving shots from a holster. She had the body of a ten-year-old boy, but the world-weary look of a veteran streetwalker, indifferent to the lecherous stares of the guys in the room.

Then I spotted a small brown-haired woman wearing a black hot-pants jumpsuit, with a neckline that plunged down to her navel. She was very petite and looked as wholesome as a college student – cute in an all-American-girl kind of way, a go-go version of Sandra Bullock, but with perkier tits and about fifteen years younger.

Tom noticed me noticing her. 'Do you want a lap dance, honey?'

'Why not?' I said. 'That would be fun, wouldn't it? For both of us.'

'You pick one, then,' he said. It was interesting that he referred to the women in such generic terms. *Pick one.* To me, there was so much variety on display.

I picked the all-American girl. Tom raised his hand and pointed at her until he got her attention. He waved her over to our table.

'Hi,' I said as she approached.

'Hi,' she replied in a cute Southern accent. Without pausing for breath, she launched a rocket. 'My name is Austin but my real name is Amy and I should tell you that I'm gay and I have a girlfriend but she's really pissed at me at the moment because I keep coming home drunk at three in the morning and she says to me, "Is there a reason why every time you come home from work, you're drunk?" and I say to her, "Honey, you try doing this job when you're sober!" '

The monologue was completely unprovoked, totally out of

the blue. I wondered if my being the only woman there gave Amy/Austin a sense of sisterly solidarity. Or maybe it was the drugs. In any case – *boom!* – the girl was off.

Tom turned to me and whispered, 'Wouldn't you just love to be this woman, just for five minutes, to see what it's like?'

It was a tempting prospect. Being a size-eight lap dancer with perky tits, a drug problem and a pissed-off girlfriend did sound like some kind of fantastic life. For five minutes.

'So, anyway,' Amy/Austin continued, 'she threw me out and said she didn't want to see me any more but I think she'll cool off in a day or two. I really love her but we have different working hours and she's a professional businesswoman and I'm doing this, although I'm just doing this until I get my real estate licence. I've got my exam in a couple weeks' time and then I want to be an appraiser and get the hell out of here, although, you know, the pay is pretty good so I can't complain.'

Tom waited for Amy/Austin to catch her breath and then said, 'Hey, my friend here would like a lap dance. Would you do that?'

'You know I'm gay?'

'Yes,' I said. 'I know you're gay. You told us somewhere along the way. It's fine. I'm liberal.'

'Great!' she said, suddenly very excited. 'Follow me.'

She led us through the club and up the stairs, to a dark narrow room which had a series of partitioned sections, each furnished with a two-seater sofa. Tom and I sat down and looked over at a man sitting opposite. He was getting a lap dance from a curvy dark-skinned woman who was naked and writhing inches away from his crotch. I wondered what Amy would do to me.

We could hear the music coming from the speakers downstairs. 'Get Ur Freak On' was playing again. The tight music rotation seemed the ultimate evidence that the focus of the club was looking, not listening.

Amy/Austin stood in front of me, rotating her hips and thrusting her little tits in the direction of my mouth, teasing me. Then she straddled my legs, facing me, and moved her lips inches from my own. Her hands moved under my dress and inched up my thigh.

'Wow,' she said when she finally touched my labia. 'No panties. Y'all are very naughty!'

I said nothing. Amy/Austin stood up and lifted my skirt. She looked at me and smiled. Then she got down on her knees and put her head between my legs and started licking my pussy. I didn't stop her.

This is a lot for twenty bucks, I thought; Tom's getting some good value here.

'Now, that's Southern hospitality,' I whispered to Tom. He said nothing, just continued watching, as did the man getting the lap dance opposite me.

I had not been with a woman since university, two decades earlier. Back at my New England college, I was known for popping straight girls' cherries. My bi phase lasted about three years and, until I realised I preferred the taste of penis, I served as the campus guinea pig for straight girls who wanted to experiment. They'd go out to a bar in the hope of scoring a stud, have too much to drink, and then, if unsuccessful, instead of stumbling back to their dorm, would knock on my door and spend the night eating my pussy.

Now here I was in Raleigh, North Carolina, in a lap-dancing club, with a stud of my own and a drunken stripper licking me out. Life had come full circle.

After five minutes or so, well past our allotted time, Amy/Austin came up for air and put her hand on my breast and her tongue down my throat. I was sure that too was against club regulations.

'Honey,' she said, 'if you're not gay, then you should be.'

I thought she was a sweet girl. Tom, meanwhile, was speechless.

Amy/Austin wasn't. She got right back to business and pumped us for another drink. 'Y'all wouldn't mind getting me another tequila, would ya?'

After that performance, I'd have bought her a whole bottle.

'She really liked you,' Tom said as we walked out the door.

'Yeah, she was cute,' I said. 'I haven't had a girl go down on me in years.'

'Well, you two really looked great together.'

'Thanks. For everything. That was fun.'

It was 1.30 in the morning. Tom drove me back to the car park and stopped his SUV next to the rental I'd hired for the week.

I leaned over to kiss my fireman as a precursor to sucking his hose. At last, he was going to get his dessert course. While we kissed, Tom pushed my dress up my waist, then bent over and put his mouth on my pussy.

'Let's move to the back seat,' I whispered after a few minutes. I didn't wait for an answer. I climbed over the front seat and into the bench in the back.

Tom followed and resumed his position between my legs. He grabbed my ankles and pushed them into the air. My legs hit the roof. It was not very comfortable, so after a few minutes I sat up and moved towards his cock. I grabbed my handbag, whipped out a condom that I'd brought along, as they say, just in case, and stretched it over his hard eight inches.

Tom drove straight into me and came in three minutes. That told me my own orgasm was out of the question.

He didn't apologise or seem bothered that I wasn't going to come, and that was OK. Tom had treated me to a nice dinner and many rounds of drinks, and he'd taken me to my first American strip club and graciously watched as a perky-titted lesbo junkie ate me out. At this point, car sex was just a bonus. To me, atmosphere and excitement carry as much weight as the fireworks.

I got back into my car, drove home to my brother's house and crept into bed. I set my alarm early, so I could make pancakes for my boys.

'So,' said Lisa the next morning, 'how was your date?'

'Oh, it was OK.'

17. THE CONTENDER

When I returned from America, I got an email from Flirtnik announcing that it had gone back online. I had been a member about a year earlier, before the site went down, and aside from my brief correspondence with Honest Jim, I hadn't logged on since. I hadn't even realised it had closed. Dating websites come and go so frequently, I can't keep track of where I'm listed. At any one time, I'm probably active on as many as five sites; and like the number of men I've slept with, I've lost count. Swinging Heaven was my mainstay, anyway.

Still, when Flirtnik informed me that, as an inaugural member, I was 'live' again, I logged in, updated my details and uploaded a fresh picture, a happy smiley jpeg featuring my new 1950s bouncy 'do and just enough cleavage not to get kicked off a trad site. I searched for men in the 38 to 55 age range, didn't see a single guy I fancied, and thought: There's a reason Swinging Heaven is so popular.

Then the next day I received an email from Honest Jim. 'You still on here?' he asked. Apparently he'd received the same 'Welcome Back' from Flirtnik. He wanted to know if I was still single. I wanted to know who he was. I just couldn't recall. A year in my romantic life is the equivalent of ten in most other women's. I receive plenty of winks from guys named Jim.

I had to dig through 63 pages of emails from hopefuls to find our ancient correspondence and his pic. Then I remembered – he was the cute guy with the crooked teeth who, after our brief online flirtation a year earlier, had gone back to his old girlfriend. I'd liked him – he'd seemed funny and smart and interested, and he'd once worked as a music buyer for a major record chain, which I thought was cool – but we'd never hooked up.

'Yes, I'm still here, Jim,' I wrote back. 'Still doing the same old things. What about you?'

He said he wasn't with his girlfriend any more and asked if I wanted to meet up. He also mentioned that he'd recently enrolled as a mature student at a London university to get his BA in English lit. I thought his desire to get a degree in his forties showed real courage. And that was a change from most of the men I met, who typically were happy to give their mind a rest and let their cock do all the thinking.

Just as I was about to update Honest Jim on my news, that I'd published the book I'd been working on a year earlier, just as I was about to say, yes, I was interested in meeting up with him, Pat called with her own news. She said that while I was in North Carolina, she'd acquired a boyfriend. They met via a bland dating site similar to Flirtnik.

'This guy really feels like The One,' she said, then began offering me a few tips on meeting guys. I thought it was funny, the amateur coaching the pro.

I let Pat dispense advice for a while, then told her about my holiday fling with the fireman. Then I mentioned I'd come home to emails from Flirtnik and had just received one from a guy I'd fancied a year earlier, who was suddenly free.

Pat suggested that, if I was going to meet him, I omit certain details of my life. 'You don't want to tell men about your book,' she said.

'Why not?'

'Well, guys on normal sites might be put off.' The word 'normal' irked me, reminding me that Pat never did quite seem to get the hook-up sites.

'But they're bound to find out, sooner or later,' I said.

'Yes, that's true, but better for them to find out on date four or five.'

'Why?' I asked. 'Just so I can postpone getting dumped?'

'No! It just gives them a chance to find out about the real you.'

'But the book *is* the real me. What's the point in their discovering that later, rather than sooner?'

Pat was convinced honesty would scare off a Flirtnik man.

'If it does, then he's not right for me,' I said.

'Trust me,' she said. 'Don't tell him. Don't!'

I thought I had nothing to lose by putting Pat's words into practice.

Despite my golden rule about avoiding conventional guys, especially after my disappointing fling-ette with Paul, I agreed to a real *date* date. On one condition. I told Honest Jim he had to dress a little better. In the updated pic he'd sent me, he was wearing khaki cargo shorts and a T-shirt that looked like something from Old Navy. It lacked originality and style. I go for men who have both.

I didn't hold out much hope for Jim. He looked too straight. Yet I liked the sound of his voice – he had a soothing tone and an unpretentious middle-class accent – and he seemed nice and interested in the world. He asked me to a Hogarth exhibition at the Tate, which made a change from asking which hotel I wanted to go to for a couple of hours. When I told him I didn't know much about Hogarth, secretly not knowing a damned thing, he gave me a charming ten-minute precis on the artist that almost made me come. I love smart guys, especially smart guys with nice voices. And I love them even more if they have a huge cock. But since we hadn't met on a swinging site, I'd have to wait to find out if Jim did.

Our schedules didn't bring us together for the art show, so instead I suggested something more to my own taste – a burlesque cabaret night called Hip Hop Hillbilly, a cheeky monthly event at the Cobden Club in West London. When I described the place to him, Jim admitted he'd never been to a burlesque club – or even, I gathered, a swingers' club, much less a fetish club – so I thought I'd break him in gently.

Part burlesque, part cabaret, part disco, Hip Hop Hillbilly had all the ingredients for a sexy evening, as the crowd was cool and at least one stripper could always be counted on to provide some titillation. The bonus was that the Cobden Club was close to where I lived, so if Jim was a disaster I wouldn't have to travel far to get home.

'The look is smart. The whole T-shirt thing,' I said, reminding him of his profile pic, 'is a real turn-off, for me anyway. I like a man who looks like a man, not like a teenager.'

'OK,' he replied, a little taken aback. 'I'll be the guy in the shell suit.'

I laughed. 'And I'll be the chick in the clingy black dress with the red cherry pattern.'

We arranged to meet at eight, when the doors opened, so we could get a good seat and, I figured, a couple of stiff drinks.

Jim was by the door when I arrived. Good start, I thought; at least this guy hasn't kept me waiting.

He was dressed in a crisp white shirt and a navy-blue double-breasted pinstriped suit. It was smart and slightly retro. He looked cute, although I could see right away the teeth were going to be problematic. They were even more scrambled than the photograph he had sent me indicated. I'm an American; good teeth are important to me.

I tried to keep in mind what Morene, my psychic, had told me a couple of years earlier – that one day I would meet and marry an older man who invested in hip, arty companies, but that it wouldn't happen until I got over some of my prejudices.

'You'll marry this man,' predicted Morene. 'This successful, creative, older man, if –' she paused for emphasis '– *if* you don't do your usual thing of discounting him first, for something minor like having bad teeth or eyes that are too close together.'

I sized up Jim. I knew that he was not rich, had a normal job with a software company and was younger than me by two years. Not the guy my psychic was referring to. But Morene was testing me. I thought that if I could get past the teeth, I might find a really great guy underneath.

'Hi,' he said, kissing me on both cheeks.

'Hi, Honest Jim. Nice suit.'

He laughed and took my arm as we walked into the club.

Hip Hop Hillbilly was fun, as usual, and so was Jim. He seemed comfortable in the place, even as the burlesque acts kicked in. And he spoke with enthusiasm about his university course and said how happy he was to be back in school after a twenty-year hiatus.

'Why'd you wait so long?' I asked.

'I had a long-term love affair that distracted me,' he said. 'With drink. Then smack.'

'I was wondering what was up with the lime and soda,' I said.

I was relieved that he didn't drink or smoke, having buried an alcoholic live-in a few years earlier and only recently jettisoned the beer-swilling Paul and the Golden Angel-guzzling Karume. It was nice to meet someone who could negotiate the world with a clear head. The only habit I was willing to put up with any more was Viagra.

Jim's eyes lit up as he told me about studying Chaucer and Shakespeare and having to write essays and do coursework again. I resisted the urge to segue from high literature to my own book. Instead, I told Jim about my day job running an entertainment company and my own nightly academics, helping my kids with their homework.

'I feel like I'm back in school, too, sometimes,' I said.

Between sets Jim and I danced to the deejay's 80s tunes. I was delighted that he could move his feet and hips to Blondie and Grace Jones and proved willing when I tried to teach him some jive steps. That was as risqué as it got between us.

Maybe Pat had a point, I found myself wondering.

We left the Cobden Club at midnight. Jim walked me back to my car and kissed me as we leaned against it. I felt his cock stiffen whilst we made out under the street lamp.

Fuck it, I thought, and reached down to touch his trousers. His cock felt large and thick as I ran my hand across his crotch.

'Nice cock,' I said, suddenly forgetting his crooked teeth and Pat's rules.

'Thanks.' Jim laughed. 'I like it.'

We kissed a bit more and then I pulled away from him. 'I better get home. I told the boys I'd be back by midnight and I'm going to be late.'

'I'll call you tomorrow, then.'

The next day he did.

'Fancy going to see a gig tonight at the 100 Club? A mate of mine is playing, and I said I'd pop by.'

'Sure, but I need to be back early,' I warned him. 'School night. I have to drop the kids off in the morning.'

The 100 Club is a legendary jazz and blues place on Oxford Street, a grotty basement venue which has hosted thousands of famous names in its half-century-plus history. I hadn't been there since my punk days, in the early 80s, when the club became notorious for hosting emerging punk and new wave bands. I wanted to see how it had changed. I also wanted to see Jim.

I called Pat to give her a progress report.

'You'll be really proud of me, Pat. I went on a date with that Flirtnik guy and I didn't talk about sex and I didn't tell him about my book, either.'

'Good girl, Suzanne!'

'Though I did grope him a little. So, how's it going with your guy?' I asked. 'When am I going to meet him?'

'Never!' said Pat, and laughed.

After I hung up, I wondered if she was joking or serious. Suddenly it occurred to me that in the four years I'd known her, Pat had never introduced me to any of the guys she was seeing. They'd never stuck around for very long, so I hadn't thought too much about it.

Just before leaving the house to meet Jim, I shot Pat an email. 'Am I being paranoid, or is there a reason you've never introduced me to any of your boyfriends?'

The blues band playing at the 100 Club was not known to me. They drew a small crowd of fifty. The music was pleasant enough, but loud, so Jim and I didn't talk much. Instead, he put his arm around me and held me close. We stayed for about an hour, then walked over to a pub on Mortimer Street for a quiet Pinot Grigio and a lime-and-soda.

At eleven o'clock, when the pub closed, Jim offered to walk me back to my car. I was parked on Wells Street, only a three-minute walk away. Jim came anyway. I couldn't walk fifty steps without him stopping to kiss me. I was amused, and also relieved, that even without going on a sex site or talking about sex on a date, I might be getting some anyway. Men are the same no matter where you find them.

'Come here,' Jim said, pulling me into the dark doorway of a closed Japanese restaurant. He wrapped his arms around my waist and pinned me against the door with his shoulders. He pressed his lips against mine, then pushed his tongue into my mouth. I felt the bulge in his jeans. Even through the heavy fabric I could make out the shape of his thick cock and feel it get harder as we kissed.

I bit gently on his bottom lip. Jim moaned and pushed his crotch closer.

'I want to taste you so badly,' he said.

I grabbed his hand and put it between my legs, guiding him towards my pussy so he could feel the wetness.

His fingers moved towards the ripe spot. He circled his finger over and around my clit, opening me up so that he could get inside. He pushed a finger into me, and then slipped it out and put it in his mouth.

'You taste delicious,' he said, smiling. 'I want to spend a lot of time down there.'

'That sounds like a really good idea,' I said. 'I'd *like* you to spend a lot of time down there. I'm glad we both agree on that.'

Jim lifted up my skirt, then crouched down on the stoop and put his head between my legs. I lifted my one and rested the heel of my stiletto on the window sill to give him more room. His tongue was gentle.

The street was dim and quiet; the only sound was my sighs.

'Ooh,' I moaned. 'That feels wonderful, wonderful.' I felt light-headed after the kissing and now the cunnilingus. I wondered if anyone living in the flats opposite the restaurant could see us. I wondered if they would get as turned on as I was.

A car drove by. Jim looked over his shoulder, then stood up.

'I don't want our first time to be like this. I want it to be special,' he said.

'C'mon,' I said, laughing. 'Let's find the car.'

Another fifty steps and another kiss. This time, Jim was more pressing. More tongue, deeper and harder in my mouth. I felt the stickiness between my legs, felt his hardness. I wished I didn't have to go home so early. I wanted to spend the night exploring Jim's body, sucking his cock, feeling him move inside of me.

Ten minutes later, we reached the car. We'd passed by it during our kiss-walk and had to double back. I unlocked the door and got into the driving seat. Jim tipped his head and smirked, indicating the passenger seat. I opened the door and he got in next to me.

'Do these seats recline?' he asked.

'These seats do everything.'

A group of young men and women spilled out of a pub and walked past us. We waited for them to move on. Then I pulled the handle at the base of the passenger seat to give Jim more room. I did the same with my seat. Jim smiled, then unbuttoned his trousers and pushed them down to his knees.

I pulled his cock out of his black boxers. I was impressed. It wasn't much longer than six inches, but it was unusually thick. The head was full and mushroom-tipped, and the thick shaft tapered down to a noticeably thicker base.

Jim put his hand around the shaft and held his cock out. I wrapped my mouth around it. I loved feeling it in my mouth, full and smooth and growing harder.

'Good,' he whispered, almost inaudibly.

We were both sober; I'd only had one glass of wine and Jim had had his usual lime-and-soda. I thought it remarkable that two completely sober people could be so completely uninhibited. I had indulged in plenty of dark-street, dark-car encounters before, but usually I was trashed and so was my partner. Tonight, it felt more real, more intimate and, in a country so steeped in alcohol, very rare.

I sucked Jim for a few minutes more. I enjoyed feeling the veins on his cock start to throb.

'Stop,' he said. 'Please. You'll make me come. I don't want to come. Not here.'

'OK.' I laughed to myself, thinking it sentimental and sweet that Jim wanted to wait. His behaviour had an almost retro vibe. We weren't virginal teenagers making out in the back seat of our parents' car after the prom. We were middle-aged adults who had lost our virginity almost three decades earlier.

Still, it meant something to wait. I realised my playtime with Jim did not have the feel of a one-night stand. But then, this should not have been a surprise to me. We'd met through a real dating website, not a swinging site. And in his profile Jim had said he was looking for a relationship, not the usual no-strings sex. If he wanted to wait, that was OK by me. I liked him. He was the kind of guy I wanted to see again. He danced well, he was up for a burlesque club, he was cute, he knew lots about music and he had a big cock. And, besides, he was Honest Jim.

I lifted my mouth from his cock. I looked into his eyes. Jim looked euphoric. He had a really hard cock and I knew he really wanted to come. The urge to fuck him was unbearable, so I moved over to Jim's seat and tried to straddle him. But the seat was too narrow and my left knee felt uncomfortable wedged against the central armrest.

I felt his hard-on press against my pussy. He put one hand on my hip and grabbed his cock with the other and rubbed the head against my labia.

I let Jim rub his cock against me for a while.

'I really don't want to do it this way,' he said at last. 'I want to be in bed with you.'

'I want to spend a whole day fucking you,' I replied. 'It's been so long since I've done that.' I'd done four-hour sessions with Christopher and breakfast bonks with Sam and group sex with Greg, but I hadn't done a full-dayer with anyone for as long as I could remember.

Then a man walked past our car and I realised how exposed we were. It brought me back to the now.

'Oops.' I laughed. I moved back over to my side of the car. We kissed some more, like on a prom date. Then I got horny. I spread my legs, resting one foot on Jim's thigh, wedging the other against the windshield. Once again Jim went down on me. And again his tongue moved around my clit and quickly got me dripping.

Suddenly car horns began beeping. A rubbish van was parked beside us, blocking traffic.

'I'm sorry,' said Jim after a third or fourth car blasted its horn. 'I find the noise a bit distracting.'

I had hardly noticed.

Jim pulled up his jeans and I rearranged my dress.

'You have a great cock,' I said, as I reached for my keys. 'I'm so glad.'

Jim laughed.

'I think we're going to fit,' I continued. 'You don't know what a relief that is.'

Jim laughed again. 'Your pussy feels tight.'

'It *is* tight,' I said. 'Pelvic exercises, tantric.'

Jim didn't know what I was talking about. I didn't explained.

'I obviously have a lot to learn,' said Jim. 'I want you to know I'm a very willing student.'

'Good. I'm sure I can teach you a lot,' I said. 'I'd like to, too.' I started up the car.

'Can you drive?' He sounded concerned.

'Of course I can drive. I only had one drink.'

'Oh, I didn't mean that,' he said. 'I'm just so light-headed now. I don't think I could drive even if I had to.'

I found his words touching. Jim was the first man who'd ever told me that sex or kissing had that effect. They did on me, as well. A great kiss can make me swoon.

'I'm fine,' I said. 'And complimented. Thanks.'

I dropped Jim off at the Ladbroke Grove tube station. I didn't want to take him to his nearby flat. I didn't want the temptation.

'I'll ring you tomorrow,' he promised.

I knew he would.

Relationships should be easy. I've always thought that if I met a guy and liked him and he liked me back, then that should be enough to get the party started. Yet it never seems to work like that for me.

My mother said that was because I'm too impulsive. I'm a sucker for the wrong things. 'You have to think of the bigger picture, Suze,' she said. Her advice came after I'd introduced her to a string of undesirables in the years after my divorce. Even before I'd noticed it myself, she'd pointed out that not one of my men had a steady job, much less a flat of his own or a car or the basic necessities of life, like money, food in the fridge or a credit card. What they did have was charisma, charm and humour. And a big cock.

Now, I found that, despite the bad teeth, I liked Jim a lot and I wanted to see him again. He was easy to talk to and smart and nice. He also met the basic requirements I'd hoped to find a man. He had a steady job and a flat and his own money in his pocket. He was also centred, level. My mother might even like him.

'I've done a lot of work on myself, Suzanne,' Jim said as I dropped him off at Ladbroke Grove. 'I don't want to lie or cheat or be dishonest. It's not my style.'

I was happy to hear those words. They were a major departure from the usual verbiage I got from boyfriend types.

The next time Jim and I saw each other, we went to dinner and a movie in Hampstead. That, as opposed to just jumping into my hot tub. I felt almost like a traditional woman and, for the first time in a long time, I liked it. I knew Jim wasn't 'The One', but I so enjoyed his company.

We were sitting in the Horseshoe pub on Heath Street when Jim said, 'I have something to tell you.'

'OK,' I said. Here goes, I thought. He's going to dump me now. Or tell me he's gone back to his girlfriend. Or maybe fess up to a STD.

'I Googled your name.' He looked sheepish.

'OK,' I said. The warning bells started ringing.

'I did it before I even met you,' he said. 'I Googled "Suzanne" and "erotic memoir" and figured out the rest.'

Suddenly I wondered if, in one of our first email exchanges, over a year earlier, I'd mentioned that I was writing a book about my sex life. I asked if this was the case and Jim said it was, and that was why he remembered me one year on.

'OK.'

'And . . .' He paused. 'And I read your book, too.'

'Uh-huh.' So much for keeping my big secret.

'And I checked out your blog and some radio interview you did a while back, and some pieces on you in the papers.'

He was beginning to sound like a stalker.

'So,' I said, 'you're saying you knew everything about me before our first date?'

'Yeah.'

'And you didn't tell me.'

'Yeah.'

'I feel kind of stupid now,' I said. 'I wouldn't have minded if you'd told me before. But half the things I told you on that first date – about my boyfriend dying and stuff – you already knew. It must have been pretty boring having to hear it all over again.'

'Well, I'm still here!' he said, as if that was a real accomplishment.

I thought about what Pat had said to me about not revealing too much before the fourth or fifth date. Jim had done his homework and worked me out before we'd even met. 'Yes, you're still here,' I said. I felt heartsick. I had wanted to open up to Jim slowly. Now, that was impossible. I wasn't Suzanne, I was someone who wrote a notorious book.

'That woman who interviewed you for the *Observer*,' he said. 'I really liked her article.'

She had said I was voracious and full of life. I'd felt complimented by her words, but Jim's words made me feel stupid.

'Yeah,' I said. 'She's a good journalist.'

I went home that night alone. I turned on the computer and checked my email. There was one from Pat in my inbox. I hadn't heard from her for a couple of days, since I'd sent her an email asking about her new boyfriend.

'You are right to be paranoid, Suzanne,' she wrote. 'I am upset with you. It struck me that I did not want to introduce you to Mike because I know that he's your "type". Don't think that you could resist flirting with him. I feel very annoyed that I do not trust you. I never will. I have come to the sad conclusion, after agonising about it, that despite your many, many fantastic qualities and all the fun we have had together, that this lack of trust has eroded my capacity to be your friend. It's bullshit to have a pal that I do not trust.'

Everybody thinks they've got me figured out, I thought. I'd never stolen anyone's boyfriend and never would. That had happened to me back in college, and it hurt for years, so I knew what it was like. But Pat was either jealous of my ease with men or paranoid. There was nothing I could do about either. What a drag to see that women who profess to be sexually liberated are threatened by women who really were.

As for Jim, I didn't know what to make of him. Either he was a groupie, a star fucker or he was simply doing his homework. You never know who you're going to meet on the web, but you do think you know your friends.

I shut off my computer and went upstairs to bed.

18. THE GANG BANG

A couple of days after our third date, Jim called to apologise for snooping on me. Then he asked me out on another date. 'I've decided. I'm not going to read your blog any more,' he said. 'What you do when I'm not around is your business.'

'OK,' I said. 'That's fine. Whatever.'

We continued to meet up every couple of weeks. Jim became what I think of as the 'boyfriend type'. That is, we met up regularly and did boyfriend–girlfriend things – movies, museums, strolls around Hampstead Heath, then always back to mine for sex.

But I wasn't his girlfriend and he wasn't my boyfriend, and that worked well for both of us.

Jim said he just wanted a rest from relationships. Then he said something that implied the opposite. 'I want to be monogamous with you, Suzanne. Do what you like. I just don't want to know.'

'You realise there's not a category for the kind of relationship you're talking about, Jim? You can't expect monogamy from someone you're not having a relationship with, especially when you don't want a relationship.'

'I'm not expecting you to be monogamous, Suzanne. I just don't want you to tell me what you get up to.'

That made a change. Most of the men I met wanted to know everything – everything about sex, that is. They got turned on hearing about my sexual escapades.

I wasn't sure I was completely comfortable with Jim's see-no-evil plan. I don't censor my conversations, as my ill-fated friendship with Pat revealed. Still, I liked Jim, and I liked having a male friend with whom I could have a moan. Since I'd stopped speaking with Pat after receiving her *sayonara* email, it was nice to have someone I could chat with about everyday things. It was also nice that he had a gorgeous cock and was fun in bed. He was a fuck buddy with benefits, only he didn't like to think of himself in those terms.

At some point, I knew, he'd find a nice, straight girl with whom he could settle down, but until that happened, I was happy to be his pit stop on the road to love.

Yet at the back of my mind was the sense that I had settled down myself. As I pondered my sex life, I came to the conclusion it had become pretty tame. My twice-monthly breakfast bonks with Sam kept the kink up. But Jim was a Flirtnik guy, and sex with him, though intimate and horny, wasn't of the tie-me-up, fuck-me-over-the-kitchen-table variety that I sometimes craved. And he was the only man I ever met who lost his hard-on when I pulled out my anal beads, and that was telling.

'What are those?' he asked, as I reached into my toy drawer.

'Anal beads.'

'What are you going to do with those?'

'Put them up my ass. What do you think?'

'Do you have to?'

'No, I don't have to,' I said. I saw that his cock was shrivelling fast, so I put the beads back in the drawer.

'What's in there?' Jim asked, looking at the stash and sounding concerned.

'My toys.'

'I've never seen a sex toy before,' he admitted.

I thought that was funny. Sam loved using me as a voodoo doll, seeing how many toys he could stick in me at once. 'Leave your toys out for me,' he often texted the night before a morning visit.

Jim wasn't into any of it. 'Do you think we can save stuff like that for another time?'

'Sure, Jim,' I said, and pulled him on top of me.

For the most part, my sex life could be summed up in three words: one on one. A breakfast boy might come over in the morning, somebody else might drop in for a long lunch and Jim might swing by at night on a kids-free weekend. Still, it was mostly one on one, and I wanted more.

I thought arranging a gang bang would break up the monotony. I also thought it would be easy to sort out. I figured all I'd have to do was put the word out to five or six of the men in my mobile, and that they'd turn up at my house on-time, cocks hard.

I'd had a gang-bang fantasy for years, but never put one together. I'd done threesomes, sucked off rows of guys in grope rooms and been in places where twenty couples were all fucking each other at once. But I'd never had a proper gang bang – that is, never been in a situation where I was the centre of attention, with half-a-dozen guys taking turns sexing me.

I really wanted a good old-fashioned kinky pounding. I wanted to turn off my brain and go to the secret place in my head set aside for pleasure, and I wanted it on my terms, which meant I wanted the men to be hot and hung.

So I sent a text to my favourite funboys, past and present:

Greg, Rump Shaker, Dr Donny, Sam, Pauli, Omar and Marcus.

'I want to have a gang bang this Friday night,' I wrote. 'Let me know if you're going to be around and if you're up for it.'

Settled. I figured even if two or three couldn't make it, that left me with enough for a proper bang.

Since Greg and I had hooked up three years earlier at Rio's, he had become a regular swinging partner, and I knew he liked a gang bang. I'd also heard through another swinging partner of his, Dawn, that he often organised parties for her, filled with half-a-dozen good-looking guys with the requisite big dicks. I figured he'd pull through for me.

Rump Shaker, another regular, ran with a pack of guys including Pauli. A year earlier, following a night of dancing at Torture Garden, I'd had a threesome with the two of them that started in my hot tub at three in the morning and finished four hours later on the sofa. I was so exhausted afterwards, I had to climb into bed alone. It was unforgettable, and not just because the sweat stains were still visible on my sofa.

Dr Donny, the horny hedge fund trader who came to my house once to play doctor, had never contacted me again. I knew he was a long shot, but though it was worth the punt. His world-class cock would be a welcome addition to the party.

Omar was a lover from a couple of years earlier and he had a massive cock. We had drifted apart. The last I'd heard from him, about six months earlier, he had a new girlfriend. But I hoped he might be tempted out of hibernation.

Finally, there was Marcus, another friend of Rump Shaker's. I'd never met him, but Carl, the Rump Shaker, had told me we might get along, if only because the two of them had the same-sized cock. He worked as a DJ and was a comedian on the side, and for fun occasionally arranged swinging parties. Our introduction was overdue, and my orgy seemed a good opportunity to bring it about.

Six hours after my texts went out, the responses began to come in.

'Hi, thanks for the invitation,' texted Sam. 'Sadly, I don't like to share. Call me selfish and greedy but waiting in a queue is not my idea of fun. X'

Then Marcus rang to say that he loved the idea but thought it best we met first for lunch. So traditional, I thought.

Omar wrote soon after to say he was getting married in three weeks time and that he didn't think going to a gang bang was such a good idea. I deleted him from my phone.

When the rest didn't respond as the day wore on, I began to doubt they would on time. I wondered what I had done wrong. Had I been too blunt? Should I have asked Greg to organise the gang bang for me? Were men supposed to take the lead? I knew Rump Shaker, for one, had recently started seeing a woman on the swinging scene, and wondered if he didn't feel right gang-banging without her. Still, that didn't explain the other guys' silence.

I had thought it would be so easy, and now I realised it wasn't going to be. As I chopped vegetables for dinner, I debated texting some of my B-list guys. Then the phone rang. It was Stephen, an artist I had met off Craigslist a few weeks earlier. He was cute, funny and sexy. We'd fucked one Saturday afternoon after lunch at the Electric and a stroll around Portobello market. We hadn't met up since then, and I had assumed he wasn't interested in me.

'How you doing?' he asked.

'Fine. Busy. Hanging out with Madonna and Gwyneth and Kate,' I joked. 'The usual.'

He laughed. 'Yes, you and your celeby world. It must be very stressful.'

I contemplated inviting him to my stress-reducing gang bang, but wasn't sure he was the kind of guy who'd go for that.

Stephen said his latest project was a painting, as a test, he wanted to do for a friend of mine who ran a gallery that specialised in animation art. He thought he might do one of Wolverine, the X-Men comic book superhero.

'My son used to collect Wolverine comics. We have a file cabinet full.'

'That's just what I need,' he said. 'Reference material.'

I offered to mail a few comics to him.

'Why do you have to send them?' said Stephen. 'Why don't you just meet me and give them to me in person?'

'OK. I'm free Saturday afternoon. Friday night might be free now, too. It all depends.'

'All depends on what?'

'I'm trying— Hold on.' I walked to the far side of the kitchen. 'I'm trying to organise a gang bang. Only I can't find anyone to come.'

'Why are you whispering?' he said.

'I don't want my kids to hear.'

'A gang bang?' Now he was the one whispering.

'Yes,' I repeated. 'A gang bang. I've never had one before. I thought it might be fun to try it out, see if I like it. It would be something different.'

'I'm afraid I can't help you there,' he said, laughing.

That was a pity. The one time Stephen and I got together, it had been unexpectedly exciting. He had a hard, athletic body and looked ten years younger than his 45 years. He was Jewish, about five foot nine, with short dark hair that was thinning on top. He wore trendy little black-framed specs that made him look like an architect or a West End advertising exec. He had on black chinos and a black T-shirt with an unbuttoned black shirt over that. I liked his fine features and intense gaze. I liked that he smiled easily. And I liked that he was Jewish. I hadn't been with a Jewish guy since I was married, and there was something comfortably familiar about Jewish guys. We shared a wry way of looking at the world.

While walking down the Portobello Road after lunch, we had stopped in some shops along the way. I bought a badge that said 'I ♥ Shoes' and another that said '100% Slut'.

'You should get one that says, "I'm a shopaholic",' Stephen said.

'I don't think so,' I said, laughing. 'I'm more of a slut.'

We drove to my house later that afternoon, got a little stoned and then fucked for two hours. I hadn't smoked a joint in four or five months, and the combination of powerful weed, Stephen's dirty grin and his perpetually hard cock really worked for me. I'd almost forgotten how great stoned sex can be.

I'd wanted him to stay the night so I could carry on fucking him. Unfortunately, I had a date in the Docklands that evening, so I kissed him goodbye in my kitchen whilst he stood there, naked, drinking a cup of tea, still hard.

He grabbed me and pulled me over and rubbed his cock between my legs. I felt myself get wet again.

As Stephen kissed me goodbye, a rush of blood went to my head. I didn't know if it was because I was stoned or because he was an especially good kisser, but I liked it. I stayed in his arms and we kissed some more.

'I'm going to make you sooooo late,' Stephen said as his cock rested at the entrance to my pussy.

'You're very naughty,' I said. 'I have fifteen minutes to make a forty-minute drive.'

Even though we had just met that afternoon, I felt I could trust him to leave the house after me. I also felt the urge to see him again. So we spoke on the phone a few times after that and tried to arrange a mutually convenient time to meet again, but we never worked it out. After a while I assumed his desire had fizzled. But now, hearing his voice again, I realised I'd rather spend the evening in bed with Stephen than getting fucked by five guys with bigger cocks.

'I could forget all about that gang bang,' I offered.

'You could.'

'I wouldn't mind the overnight.'

'Well, I'll have to check if Friday is OK,' Stephen said. He paused for two seconds. 'As it so happens, I'm free.'

'So, I'll see you Friday night. You can go through the comic books, then you can come to bed,' I said. 'The gang bang is officially off.'

I texted the other guys to call off the gang bang.

Stephen came round Friday after work for another night of grass, kisses and orgasms. I forgot all about the gang bang.

For almost twenty-four hours. Then on Saturday afternoon Greg rang.

'You around this evening?'

'Yes, I'm around. What do you have in mind?'

'I was thinking about Dunstable,' he said. He was referring to Arousal, a popular swingers' club in Bedfordshire, 45 minutes up the M1 from London. 'Wanna go?'

'Sure,' I said. 'Why not?'

'Pick you up at ten.'

I'd never been to Arousal but had heard plenty, first from Relish Man in the steam room at Rio's and later from Rump Shaker Carl, who had invited me to join him on several occasions. Carl made the club sound like the sexiest play palace in the UK, but I wasn't convinced. Any handsome guy with a ten-inch cock is going to have fun wherever he goes.

Thinking Carl might want to join us, I called him up and invited him and his partner to make it a foursome.

'Lovely, Suzanne. We were planning on going anyway,' he said. 'We'll phone you when we're on our way.'

Greg arrived at my house dressed in his standard party outfit – black T-shirt, black jeans, black leather jacket, black leather cap.

I'd set my hair in a 50s bob, my now-favourite style, and put on a vintage 50s dress that enhanced the retro look. It was a blue silk sleeveless number with an empire waist that flared out, very different from the standard black-lace nighties I knew would adorn most of the women there. Underneath, I wore a new Agent Provocateur pale-peach set, bought for me by a 27-year-old Craigslist admirer who got off on buying me lingerie after watching me try it on in the dressing room.

The bra, panties and suspender belt were almost transparent, but frilly enough to cause a stir. As soon as I'd stepped into them that night, I felt my sex drive boost a notch. Expensive lingerie turns me on. I hoped it would affect the men at Arousal in the same way. I slipped on my usual fishnet stockings and black patent fuck-me shoes to complete my look.

'Wow,' said Greg when I opened the door.

I laughed. 'Thought I'd make an effort. I want a gang bang tonight.'

In the past I had declined Rump Shaker's invitations to Arousal because I hadn't seen the point of making such a long journey for sex when plenty was available right in London. But I was horny and determined to have more than one cock that night and I knew I could count on Greg to round up a few guys.

Greg drove and, like a homing pigeon, reached his destination, pulling into a row of garages just behind a suburban residential street. Had I not been chauffered, I never would have found it. Greg drove the car down a narrow gravel road and pulled into the last available spot, at the end of a row of some twenty other vehicles.

'Looks like a busy night,' I said, cheered.

We walked into the club and up the stairs to reception. It was dark and basic, no décor. Somehow, instantly deflating. The woman sitting behind the window put us through the usual newbie routine: fill out a form, present picture IDs, pay the entrance fee. Then she told us to follow her, for the guided tour.

'I'm Joan,' she said. 'Let me show you around.'

She was blonde, middle-aged, overweight and well endowed. Her skimpy black Ann Summers lace lingerie barely contained her big tits. She had all the cheeriness of an old-fashioned tea lady.

Guided tours of swingers' clubs is de rigueur for first-timers. The ritual helps a hostess make her guests feel comfortable and helps guests earmark the best spots for playing. The top swinging clubs are usually run by people who are in the lifestyle themselves, and their pleasure in their work usually shows. Joan was as cheery and knowledgeable as any other long-time player.

'Now this,' she said, pointing to the main room, 'is the chill-out zone. There's a bar over there –' she gestured to the right – 'for you to put your wine and spirits. You can buy mixers and crisps, too.'

Greg walked over to the bar with the blue carrier bag he'd brought. He handed the bartender two bottles of Grolsch. I always went to clubs carrying a flask filled with freezing-cold vodka, but kept it with me, in my handbag.

Joan took us down a hallway that led to a tiny black room, perhaps three-feet by three, with a small black cushion on the floor and Styrofoam blocks each cut into the shape of a rock or a crater, painted grey, and glued to the ceiling.

'This is the cave,' she said. I stared at the lone cushion on the floor and made a mental note to avoid that space. It looked like a leftover from a primary-school production of a caveman skit, comical, not sexy.

Continuing the tour, Joan led us through a labyrinth of rooms. There was a cinema playing triple-X videos, with a balcony above for voyeurs, plus a dark room, a grope room, a couples' playroom. There were separate bedrooms with lockable doors, a dance floor with a pole set-up on a stage to serve a girl's go-go fantasy, and a mock castle to – I didn't know what. It was a regression to the playschool theme.

'This place looks like it's been put together with sticky tape and plasterboard,' I whispered to Greg.

He laughed. 'Don't lean against the walls. They might fall down.'

Though I had lost my way ten minutes earlier, eventually we came full circle and ended up back in the main room. There seemed to be doors everywhere and I couldn't figure out where any of them led. I wondered if Carl and his girlfriend were behind one of them.

'Well, should we get started?' I asked Greg.

'Sure.'

'You lead the way. I haven't got a clue.'

We took a gamble and walked through one of the many doors. We were back at the cinema. A couple was sitting close together on one of the sofas, hands on each other's thighs, watching the screen.

'What about the balcony?' said Greg.

We walked past the couple and up the steps that led upstairs. A bed-sized foam pad covered in vinyl fabric was positioned against one wall. A sofa was set against it, facing the cinema screen. I climbed on the platform and hitched up my skirt, displaying the top of my suspenders. Greg stood in front of me, slowly unzipped his fly and pulled out his cock. I put my arms around his buttocks and pulled him closer. I took him inside my mouth and felt him get harder, whilst my tongue rode up and down the length of his shaft.

'That's right,' he said. 'Use your tongue. Use your tongue.'

I pressed my tongue firmly against the shaft, pulling his cock deep into my mouth.

'That's a girl. Pull it in. All the way.'

I loved following Greg's orders. I moved my mouth slowly down his cock and tried to reach its thick base. I gagged.

'Good girl,' he said.

I pulled out to catch my breath. I looked around. An attractive thirtyish couple had moved onto the sofa to watch. A lone man, mid-thirties, slim, dark-haired, stood next to them, wanking in silence. I ignored our audience and turned back to Greg. I took his cock in my mouth and felt him get harder.

I pulled out and licked the head of his cock. I ran my tongue along the shaft, then wrapped my hand around it and began sliding my hand up and down.

After five minutes, I felt him convulse, felt the warm stream of his come shoot down my mouth. Greg continued to tremble for a half-minute more while resting his cock in my mouth.

'Next?' I said after releasing Greg's cock. I looked over at the solitary man who had been wanking. 'What are you waiting for?' I said.

He walked over to me and put his cock in my mouth. He wasn't as big or as thick as Greg, but sucking on Greg's nine-inch cock had made me horny. Now I wanted to be fucked, simple as that. I pulled a condom out of my handbag, ripped open the wrapper and stretched it over the guy's shaft. Then I turned around, got on all fours and hitched up my dress, presenting my ass to him.

Without a word, he slipped inside my wet pussy and fucked me. He came and exited in minutes. It didn't matter. I wanted to wait for my own orgasm, preferably with Greg, and preferably back at my place later. Arousal was just extended foreplay for me.

After the stranger pulled out of me, I turned around and he leaned towards me. We kissed.

'Thank you,' he said. 'That was amazing.'

'You're welcome,' I said. 'Next.'

Another man had appeared during the fucking and was standing against the wall. He walked over to me and unzipped his trousers. Once again, I took a cock in my mouth and once again I brought it to completion.

'Well done,' said Greg, cheering me on.

'Let's look around,' I said. 'I think it's time for my gang bang, don't you?' I straightened my clothes and got off the platform. 'Thanks, guys,' I said to the two strangers, who'd each taken turns watching the other perform with me. 'That was fun.'

They smiled.

As I walked down the stairs, I removed the flask from my handbag and took a swig of vodka. The cold liquid soothed my throat. Greg and I worked our way through the labyrinth of doors and passages back to the bar.

'Number seventeen,' Greg said to the bartender, a bald man in a PVC vest and trousers.

'Well, that was horny,' I said.

'Very.'

We stood in silence, looking around the main room. It had filled up since we'd arrived only an hour earlier. There were seven or eight couples, a range of types. There were also two women who looked to be in their thirties sitting together on a sofa. I wondered if they were gay or just two rare women who'd made the jump from dating site to sex club. Most women at swingers' clubs entered on the arm of a guy. And it was rare to see lesbians in a swingers' club. The scene was a mostly heterosexual one, as an entire constellation of clubs and saunas serve an exclusively gay clientele. A bi vibe was often in the air in swingers' clubs, especially among women or in group scenes that involved a lot of body contact in tiny spaces. Bi women were particularly welcome, bi men less so.

I'd have welcomed a bit more guy-on-guy action in the clubs, as I found it a major turn-on, but as Greg once told me, 'Some guys hate it when I manoeuvre their cock into position with my hands.' Greg isn't bi; to him, a cock was just a cock, a piece of equipment. If another guy's cock needed moving to facilitate its entry into a woman he was fucking, then he didn't have a problem steering it towards another hole. It wasn't sexual touch so much as a practical manoeuvre.

I looked around the room once more at all the faces, trying to see if I could match the men with the cocks I had just sucked. It had been dark on the balcony, and I hadn't really paid too much attention to the faces. I have never had a good memory for faces.

'Do you want to have another walk around?' I asked Greg when he finished his Grolsch.

'Sure.' Greg was always up for a new adventure.

We walked around the club and stopped at a large room with mirrors on the ceiling, pausing to look through a long window cut into a wall. Three couples were fucking. One man had his finger between his partner's legs. Another was lying on his back and being straddled by his partner. A third couple were masturbating each other. A group of men stood alongside us, watching the action.

'Boring,' I said.

We carried on to the dark room. Three men were playing with a woman hidden from our view. But we could hear her moans and the sound of a heavy cock slapping against flesh. Her thigh? His palm? I couldn't tell, but it was erotic.

Then we came to a small square room. It was empty except for a square bed that fitted snugly inside. It allowed for a spare metre on three sides for people to watch or play with their bedmates.

'This looks good,' I said. I put my handbag to one side and pulled out my essentials: my leopard-print bullet vibe, some lube, a blindfold and some condoms.

I removed my dress, put on the blindfold and lay down on the bed. I left on my peach lingerie and black heels.

'Get on all fours,' Greg said.

I heard trousers unzip. I felt Greg's hands reach behind my head. He pushed his sweaty cock into my mouth again.

'That's right,' he said. 'All the way down.'

I felt him get harder. Another set of hands reached between my legs and began to massage my clit. Greg was holding on to both sides of my head, using my mouth like a sex toy, pushing it up and down his cock.

'You can fuck her if you want,' I heard him say.

I removed my mouth when I felt a new cock against my ass. 'Is there a condom on that thing?'

'Yes,' said an unfamiliar voice. I liked his baritone.

I felt around for Greg's cock and pulled him back into my mouth. Then I felt a cock straining against my pussy, then finally sliding in, all the way in. The blindfold accentuated every sensation: my mouth against a cock; a cock moving inside my pussy.

Someone's hand cupped my breast. It could have been Greg's or a stranger's; it was hard to be sure. I couldn't be sure of anything. Hands and cocks and lips and tongues touched me. Different cocks entered me. After twenty, thirty, forty minutes I couldn't tell who was who or how many there had been. And I didn't care.

Then I heard Greg say, 'Get on your back.'

I rolled onto my back, as commanded, bent my knees and spread my legs.

'Come here,' said Greg, as he pulled my thighs towards him.

I felt a well-lubed cock prodding my asshole.

'Slow,' I whispered, although I knew I didn't have to say anything. In the three years I'd known him, Greg had gotten to know my body as well as I knew it myself. I felt safe with him in the square room. I knew he would look after me. And, as anal was his big turn-on and he was well travelled, I knew I didn't have to coach him.

Yet the thing about being blindfolded is that you can never be one hundred per cent sure of anything. It is an instinctive response to caution slowness, even though I knew it was Greg pulling my ass to his cock, even though he always took anal slowly and knew I needed to relax first.

I felt a sudden push against my sphincter. I took in breath deeply, letting the oxygen course deep into my lungs to speed up the endorphin rush.

'The head's in,' he said quietly.

'Slow,' I said again, unnecessarily, relaxing my muscles so they'd open up to give way to his thick cock. 'Wait.'

Once again I took in deep breaths. I felt the muscles relax. Greg pushed – an inch, another inch – until finally, after five long minutes, he was deep inside me.

There could have been a hundred people in that room, but it felt like just the two of us. I relaxed and let Greg fuck me until I was wide open, taking him over and over again, deeper and deeper inside my ass.

'Oh, God,' I moaned.

'God has nothing to do with this,' he said. 'I'm fucking you up the ass.'

I laughed.

'Take off your blindfold,' he said.

I removed the blindfold. I saw a circle of hard cocks hovering above my head, their owners stroking them.

I opened my mouth and raised my head to receive their come. The stroking became more frantic.

I heard Greg's breath quicken. He started panting. Then I felt the rush of his spunk inside me. As he let out a huge groan, the wanking above my face ceased. The men in the circle paused to watch the guy with the huge cock come.

I let Greg relax in my ass. His cock softened. He stopped thrusting into me. Somehow that signalled the end for all of us. Greg slid out of me and the circle of jerkers broke up. The guys put their cocks back in their pants and, one by one, walked out of the room. The show was over.

I sat up and pulled on my clothes. Greg and I were alone.

'Come on, honey, let's go home,' I said. 'You can fuck me properly there.'

We drove back to London, both really turned on by our night up the M1. Greg had one hand on the steering wheel, the other on his dick. I reached over to play with his balls and with my other hand held my leopard-print vibrator against my clit.

'Do you realise we've been doing this shit for three years now?' I said.

'Yeah, it's great, isn't it?' Greg laughed. 'Not bad for a couple of middle-aged pervs.'

We parked in front of my house, then went straight up to my bedroom and had an old-fashioned screw. Greg took me on my knees, stuck his big cock in my ass for the second time that night, and very slowly slid in and out. I finally got my big orgasm, and Greg got his third. We both slept soundly afterwards.

'It doesn't get better than this,' I said to Greg when we woke up the next morning. I realised I'd used that expression before, in similar situations. But it was true. It really doesn't get any better.

'You're right, Suzanne,' Greg said. 'It doesn't get any better.'

He rolled towards me and put his arm around my waist.

I lay in bed, thinking about the men who'd come into my life in the years since my divorce. I knew I wasn't ready for another relationship. I was having too much fun to even want one. Still, I knew eventually I'd meet someone who wanted to grow old with me. Someone like Greg – a guy with whom I could share adventures and who shared my desire to sometimes run free. I didn't know when this man would come into my life, but I knew he was out there.

I put my arm around Greg, drew him near and went back to sleep.